OTHER BOOKS BY SEAN DUNN

I Want the Cross
Know Him, Serve Him
Velocity

momentum

:: GAINING GROUND WITH GOD ::

sean dunn

Fleming H. Revell
A Division of Baker Book House Co
Grand Rapids, Michigan 49516

Published by Fleming H. Revell
a division of Baker Book House Company
P.O. Box 6287, Grand Rapids, MI 49516-6287
www.bakerbooks.com

Printed in the United States of America

Library of Congress Cataloging-in-Publication Data
Dunn, Sean, 1968-
   Momentum : gaining ground with God / Sean Dunn.
        p.   cm.
   ISBN 0-8007-5912-5 (pbk.)
   1. Teenagers—Religious life. 2. Teenagers—Conduct of life. 3. Spiritual life—Christianity. I. Title.
BV4531.3.D866 2004
248.8′3—dc22   2003022337

contents

introduction

i like it at the top!

UMPFFF! It was all I could do to control the stomach that was trying to come through my mouth. First of all, I couldn't believe I'd gotten talked into getting onto a roller coaster that made me queasy just looking at it. And second, I was embarrassed that I was struggling to handle it.

As I sat on the coaster next to one of my best friends, I tried to look like I was enjoying the ride, but it was all a facade. I hated it. Every swerve, curve, hill, and dip was making my stomach churn and my smile disappear. And we had yet to approach the halfway point of this ride.

Not recognizing the danger that potentially awaited him, my friend leaned over and excitedly said, "Isn't this great?" Trying to sound sincere, I responded, "Sure."

As we came around a mild curve and began to climb to the highest point on the coaster, I finally relaxed a little. But that was when I saw them—the corkscrews. Six of them in a row! Panic hit my heart. Tears came to my eyes. I wanted out, but there was no way.

As we reached the pinnacle of the hill, the cars seemed to almost stop. For just a moment we weren't going up and we weren't going down. But I knew that it wouldn't last. I hadn't made it to safety yet; the descent was just about to begin.

Slowly at first, then rather quickly, the coaster came off the peak and moved toward the loops. My friend's hands were raised in the air, his face was glowing with excitement, and his mouth was screaming in exaltation, but not me. My hands were glued to the safety bars across my chest. My face had a panicked look on it (I know this because I was able to see a picture in the gift shop after the ride), and my eyes and mouth were shut.

For the next sixty to ninety seconds, I held on for dear life, hoping and praying that the whipping and whirling would stop. It finally did. We lurched to a stop at the dock we had left just a few minutes before.

Disoriented, I crawled out of the little car I had put my trust in and started down the ramp. Finding a bench, I sat down and tried to regain control of my head and stomach. My friend joined a couple other people to tackle another coaster, but I chose to sit it out. I needed a break.

THE ROLLER COASTER OF LIFE

The friend with me that day was Zach. And it's ironic that he was the one who shared that experience with me, because Zach didn't just ride roller coasters, he lived them.

For about two years of our lives, we did everything together — that's why he could talk me into something like that. We met when we were about seven years old, and although we had similar backgrounds (Christian homes, solid church, and Christian friends), we lived very different lives. Zach lived a series of ups and downs in his faith, his relationships, and his emotions.

On the roller coaster that day, I felt that I had no control as the metal rails took the car I was riding in up, down, and around. In his life, Zach felt that he had no control. Sometimes his anger would rise up and explode onto the scene without any warning. And other times his depression was so deep that he could barely have a conversation.

Spiritually, he had annual cycles, visiting the mountaintops of commitment only to fall quickly to the depths of the valley. His decisions to follow God were sincere, yet he struggled to live them out. He really wanted to walk closely with God, but there were some things standing in the way. He kept tripping along the way and hitting walls.

Although I would love to tell you that he overcame those things and is walking closely with God today, that is not true. Either Zach never discovered what caused his struggles, or he wasn't willing to take drastic measures to reduce their drain on his life. I don't know why, but I know that he is now in his thirties and still on a roller coaster.

DO YOU WANT TO GO FOR A RIDE?

Let's face it: We are not all alike. Some people like roller coasters, and some would rather avoid them. Although you may be different from me, when I was growing up, I didn't enjoy things that scared me.

I know you might have made fun of me if you had seen me on the roller coaster that day. You might have pointed, laughed, and mocked because I was a wimp. I couldn't handle a simple roller coaster.

However, I refuse to point and laugh at you if you find yourself on a roller coaster like the one my friend Zach has lived on since he was a boy, because there's absolutely nothing funny about it.

There's nothing humorous about the embarrassment that comes from disappointment or the anguish that comes from failure. I never laugh when I see someone struggling to figure out how to live consistently and walk with God.

If you have been on a frustrating ride, are you ready to get off? Are you tired of the roller coaster? Do you want to experience some stability? Well, then it's time you recognize the dips and valleys and work to avoid them.

EXPOSING THE DROP-OFFS

As I rode the coaster with Zach that day, I actually enjoyed one thing about the journey. I had a great time on the climbs.

When the coaster started moving upward with slow and deliberate momentum, I was having fun. The pace was just right, there was no imminent danger, and the view got better with each click of the rails. However, instead of allowing you to stay at the summit, roller coasters are built to force you back toward the ground where the views are ordinary and the movements are uncomfortable.

The same is true of our spiritual journey. When we are climbing toward God and our path has set us on a course toward growth, we feel good. The view is great. As our eyes are directed heavenward, we see God and everything else in a balanced perspective. This is the adventure God intended us to live and enjoy.

However, the enemy of our souls will sneak in and work to turn our path downward. If we don't pay attention and we refuse to let God direct our course, our lives turn into true roller coasters.

The purpose of this book is to show you how to avoid some of the dips that lie in the path of every Christian. I can't deal with every tactic the devil may use to knock you off your peak, so I'm going to focus on four major areas:

"Minor" Sins That Demand Major Attention
Explosive Emotions
Addictions
Social Issues

If you want to stop the trends that lead to major setbacks in your faith, you must let God help you expose the things that tend to trip you up and show you how to walk free from them. This takes courage, discipline, and prayer. But it's worth it—unlike my ride on the real roller coaster, you can stop the roller coaster ride of your life whenever you choose to.

ARE YOU READY?

As you begin this journey of self-examination and letting God inspect you, hold on and don't squirm. If God begins to reveal truth to you in an area that is uncomfortable, don't fight it. As God exposes the areas where you have struggled, he will help you bring those things into proper balance.

Keep your hands and feet inside the car at all times. It's time to climb!

GAINING GROUND

Ask Yourself This—Are you willing to let God challenge you and speak to some difficult areas in your life? Which of the four areas that will be discussed in this book do you believe will apply to you the most? I'm convinced that this is going to be a difficult book for many people to read because it's very direct and speaks to some of the hidden areas of your life. You'll be willing to walk through it with honesty and prayer only if you're truly surrendered to God and want his will more than your own. Are you at that place in your journey of faith?

Key Scripture — "Flee the evil desires of youth, and pursue righteousness, faith, love and peace, along with those who call on the Lord out of a pure heart" (2 Tim. 2:22).

Ask God to Help — As you begin this book, you need to take an inventory of your life and make sure that every area is submitted to God. If you really are in that place, then your journey is about to get interesting. You can lay everything in God's hands by praying this prayer: *"Lord Jesus, I come to you today as someone who isn't perfect. I struggle, but I want to walk closely with you. Lord, I give you every part of me and ask that you work in my life. I won't hold anything back, but I will give you complete access. You can talk to me about anything, and I will respond to you. Thank you for loving me and for helping me avoid the things that would make me stumble. I can't wait to live the rest of my life with you and for you. Amen."*

"minor" sins that
Demand major
attention

I

if you tell one lie, does that make you a liar?

When Brandon was finishing his freshman year of high school, some people mercilessly teased him about not having a girlfriend. After several weeks of defending himself from their taunting and name-calling, he decided to deflect the attention. So he made up an elaborate scheme and put it into practice that summer.

When school resumed after two and a half months of recess, Brandon had a girlfriend. Excitedly he told everyone who would listen that he had met Tasha over the summer while he was visiting his grandparents' house on the east coast and they had fallen in love. As he flaunted the relationship he'd invented, everyone around was impressed.

Recognizing that his hoax was not only successfully deflecting the persecutions that he had recently endured, but also winning the admiration of his peers, he kept building on the foundation. He found some pictures of a dark-haired beauty and deemed her Tasha. He shared stories of their conversations and willingly shared of her undying love for him. He even wrote letters, saying they were from her, which he laced with beautiful-smelling perfume.

She seemed like the perfect girl. After all, every tale was carefully constructed to make Brandon look like the "stud muffin" who'd won the beauty.

However, by the middle of his junior year, he'd gotten lost in the game. What he had begun to avoid embarrassment became the defining part of his life. Rarely did he have conversations in which Tasha didn't come up. And he could never let his guard down for fear that he would be caught in his web of deceit.

However, that all changed one Wednesday night. After a youth service Brandon approached me and pulled me aside. "Sean," he said, "I've been living a lie." He proceeded to tell me about the elaborate way he had been lying to everyone in his life. He looked at me and said, "It's too much. I can't do it anymore. From this moment on, I refuse to lie about it anymore. Sean, you're the first, but I'm going to tell everyone that Tasha isn't real."

Because I knew how hard this was for him, I encouraged him by telling him I was proud of him for getting this out in the open. And I told him that he was doing the right thing. I asked if he would like it if I prayed with him, and he said he would. So in the corner of the youth room, I put my hand on his shoulder and asked God to give him the strength to get free from his lie and to protect him from the people who were going to harass him for lying to them for so long. As soon as I said amen, Brandon began to make his way around the room, telling people one by one that he had been living a lie.

RECOGNIZE THE DROPS

Society doesn't value truthfulness. Instead, it values image and self-protection. Therefore, in some people's eyes, it's okay to lie if it enhances others' perception of you or if there is some definite advantage to telling a lie in that moment. However, the people who believe this don't share God's opinion on the subject.

On some unseen level we struggle to understand the severity of bending the truth, and we fail to embrace honesty as the best policy. As a matter of fact, although most are taught from an early age that "Thou shalt not lie," many toil with the thought. That's why so many (even Christians) lie habitually. They do it often and they do it well.

There are several different ways people lie. Some of them are more obvious than others. And while some are easier to justify, all forms of deceit are sin.

ways people lie

The flagrant mistruth. Did you know that even young children have a tendency to lie? It amazes me that they seem to have little conscience in the matter. They will say whatever comes to their minds if it is to their advantage. Dad will ask, "Did you clean your room like I told you to?" Instead of speaking the truth—"No, Dad. I was playing and forgot."—they say what is most to their advantage: "Yes, Dad, I did."

Many have mastered flagrant mistruth. There is absolutely no sense of reality in anything they say.

The bent truth. Although there is some sense of accuracy, by leaving out certain details, people can manipulate the circumstances for their gain.

The unspoken lie. The unspoken lie is a tool that many people are able to rationalize. "Well, I never actually said that," they say as they refute the claim that they lied. However, they willingly and knowingly allowed a person to walk away from a conversation believing a certain thing that wasn't true. They didn't speak the lie, but they didn't speak the truth either. Bottom line: Intent is key. If they allowed something that wasn't true to hang out there and be adopted as true, then they lied.

The gifted exaggeration. Some of the people in my life who have captured my attention as chronic liars weave this type of lie very well. They can take an ounce of truth and build a grand story around it, making it bigger than life. They can contribute to conversations, claiming everything they say to be valid when it ends up being completely fictitious. They can build complex legends around one statement or action, enlarging the rest of the story for effect or laughter.

Again, some would defend their exaggerations and claim them not to be lies; however, many times they prove to be just that.

A life of fiction. Like Brandon, some people live a life of fiction rather than telling an occasional tale. Parts of their backgrounds are made up. What they know, who they know, and what they have done are all fabricated rather than factual.

This scenario has been famously played out in recent years by media personalities. The stories of their lives have been proven false as the truth comes to the forefront.

One of the saddest things to watch is when people live their lies for so long that they forget who they truly are.

reasons people lie

For protection. On occasion the truth is not popular because an untruth is less incriminating. No one wants to admit that they made a mistake, so it's easier to pretend to not know who spilled the milk or put the scratch on the car.

It's a rare person who is willing to stand up and admit responsibility, but people who want to be Christ-like understand that this kind of maturity is a choice. And it's those people who won't hide from the truth.

Image enhancers. Simply put, many people lie to make themselves look better than they are. Whether they're exaggerating about their athletic accomplishments or fabricating a story about their social lives, their ultimate goal is to be the center of attention and to impress everyone present.

They sacrifice God's command to live truthfully, because their insecurities have convinced them that their lives aren't exciting enough or they aren't good enough on their own. The ironic thing is that these lies have a tendency to explode, leaving the teller of the lie embarrassed and disgraced.

Lack of courage. Some people lack the courage to tell the truth. "Yes, Mom, I deliberately disobeyed you. That is why I'm late," is more difficult to say than, "Mom, my car wouldn't start."

It takes guts to tell the truth when you know it's going to produce consequences.

Flattery. Flattery is visible from miles away, and very rarely does it sound authentic. However, many people weave words of adulation like they were going out of style. "Amy and I were just talking about you. We think you are absolutely the nicest person in the world." "I don't know what your team would do without you. You hold it all together out there."

Although there are people who truly are encouragers and are authentic in their compliments, there are also those who use deceptive flattery as a tool to manipulate friendships instead of earning them.

God wants us to be positive people who look for visible ways to love and affirm others, but in your desire to do that, don't use empty words to flatter people.

Is there a problem here? Yes. By simple observation I've discovered that there are not that many people who see truth as a priority.

Although there is a lack of truthfulness in our culture, if anyone is going to trumpet the mandates and benefits of speaking the truth, then it must be Christians. God has commissioned us to walk in truth, to articulate it, and to demonstrate it. It must be a priority in our communication and in our lifestyle. We must not accept our lies anymore.

LEARN GOD'S APPROACH

God's opinion is very clear in the Bible. We need only to look in Scripture to discover how zealous God is for the truth and how much he opposes deceit.

> "Into your hands I commit my spirit; redeem me, O LORD, the God of truth" (Ps. 31:5). God is truth. His power is based in truth. He relates to his creation truthfully and honestly.

"Surely you desire truth in the inner parts; you teach me wisdom in the inmost place" (Ps. 51:6). Because God's nature is truth, it is what he desires and what he teaches. His truth leads to wisdom.

"These are the things you are to do: Speak the truth to each other, and render true and sound judgment in your courts" (Zech. 8:16). God commands us to speak the truth to each other.

"You belong to your father, the devil, and you want to carry out your father's desire. He was a murderer from the beginning, not holding to the truth, for there is no truth in him. When he lies, he speaks his native language, for he is a liar and the father of lies" (John 8:44). The devil is the father of all lies. All deceit comes from him. For this reason, we must walk in, cling to, and speak the truth.

"Jesus answered, 'I am the way and the truth and the life. No one comes to the Father except through me'" (John 14:6). Jesus is the truth. You'll never find him in a lie.

"But when he, the Spirit of truth, comes, he will guide you into all truth. He will not speak on his own; he will speak only what he hears, and he will tell you what is yet to come" (John 16:13). The Holy Spirit is based in truth, and he leads us into all truth. There is no deception in him.

"For you were once darkness, but now you are light in the Lord. Live as children of light (for the fruit of the light consists in all goodness, righteousness and truth) and find out what pleases the Lord" (Eph. 5:8–10). Deceit is characteristic of someone who is living in spiritual darkness. But one of the indicators that we are living in the light is that we walk and speak truthfully. And this is one of the things that pleases the Lord.

"Do not lie to each other, since you have taken off your old self with its practices and have put on the new self, which is being renewed in knowledge in the image of its Creator" (Col. 3:9–10). Lying is associated here with the life that has yet to find Christ. Once we have found him, we are to live differently. Dishonesty must disappear as we walk closely with God.

IT'S TIME TO CLIMB

Lies are a trap. Instead of working on behalf of the one shading the truth, many times they end up attacking the one telling the story. Lies either expose them immediately or hold them hostage for fear that the truth will be discovered.

In the long run, nothing good comes from dishonesty. When reality is distorted, it damages relationships, destroys confidences, and devastates trust. For that reason, it is imperative that you denounce lies and choose to walk in truth. Here are a few suggestions to help you move in that direction:

Change your heart. The Bible teaches us that if your mouth lies, it is a heart condition (see Matt. 12:34), not simply a random action. That doesn't mean that your heart doesn't belong to God; it means that some portion of your heart is embracing deceit. Therefore, to break free from lying, you must give more of your heart over to the truth of God and his Word.

By taking time to bring the Word of God into your life and by letting the presence of God saturate your heart, dishonesty will begin to lose its grip.

Lying isn't simply a social choice; it's a spiritually influenced habit. Because of that, you must attack it on a spiritual plane. To overcome it, you must go to its source. You must pray for, do surgery on, nurture, and change your heart.

Recognize when you tend to lie. Are there certain people you tend to lie to the most? Are there certain situations that tend to make you avoid the truth? If you recognize them, you will have an upper hand on the problem. By observing your habits, you may begin to see patterns. That, along with the fact that you are desperately working to alleviate these practices, will give you an edge that will go a long way toward winning this battle.

Beg God to help you hate your lies. Lying comes naturally because we like the lies more than we like the truth. That's why we need to learn to hate our lies. Only when we begin to hate them for what they do to us (force us to live in darkness, always hiding, always afraid that we'll be discovered), will we work toward freedom.

Let it be known—God hates your lies! Because he hates them, he wants you to hate them as well. It's good to pray that God would help you overcome your lies. But you can also take it one step further. Ask God—no, *beg* God—to help you hate any lie that wants to influence your life or come out of your mouth.

Embrace the truth. Although most people wouldn't define it as a discipline, that is what truth is all about. It's about choosing to live the truth, speak the truth, believe the truth, and share the truth. It takes discipline to master the art of telling the truth, but if you embrace it (meaning you commit with everything you have to walk in truth), then you will be victorious.

God is on your side. He is right there with you, offering you all of his ability, strength, and power to live in the truth, so if you radically choose to embrace only the truth, then together you and God can master this part of your life.

Promise to admit lies immediately. Although nothing else seemed to work for some students, when they promised God that they would confess their lies as soon as they recognized they had spoken them, they began to lie less often.

Something about going to a friend, parent, teacher, or pastor and admitting that they had lied began to scare them straight. They didn't want the humiliation of sharing their sin with those people, so they had a better ability to recognize the lie before it slipped out into the open.

If you're serious about removing deceit from your life, then you'll make this same commitment. Before God and with someone you respect in the Lord, you can commit to expose every lie you speak. I promise you that this will bring about some changes in how frequently you allow lies to float out of your mouth.

VIEW FROM THE TOP

This topic is especially meaningful for me because it is one of the major battles I had as I was growing up. As a young Christian, I struggled to tell the truth. Lies came to me more easily and more often. I lied so much in my early teens that I stopped feeling guilty about it.

After years of lying daily, that all began to change. God began to convict me and move inside my heart. I realized that he has a standard of truthfulness that I needed to work toward. I recognized that in God's eyes I couldn't rationalize any amount of duplicity. As the conviction grew in my heart, I knew I couldn't continue to rationalize my sin. I had to overcome it.

After months of working hard to speak the truth, I was failing. I was becoming discouraged. Finally, when I thought I would never overcome my addiction to dishonesty, I discovered the remedy. I realized that I had to change my heart.

Up to that point, I'd been trying to conquer my habit, to change my actions, but I was ignoring my heart. And I was trying to do it on my own without God's help. Out of desperation more than anything else, I began to pray and ask God to assist me in my fight. And I began to read the Bible daily. Now, I realize that these actions don't sound revolutionary, but I can tell you they proved to be effective. My lying began to diminish. My tongue came under control.

After a few months, I looked back at my life and realized that although I hadn't become perfect, I had learned to be more truthful. I invited God to assist me, and I allowed the Word of God (100 percent truth) to encounter my deceit. Truth won out.

And truth can win out in your life too. It must.

GAINING GROUND

Ask Yourself This—Do you have a problem with lying? When was the last time you let a lie slip out of your mouth? Are there people in your life you tend to lie to on a regular basis? Is lying a sin? Do you believe that it's ever acceptable? If you struggle with lying, what steps are you going to take to overcome this habit? Were you tempted to lie about the answers to any of these questions?

Key Scripture—"Surely you desire truth in the inner parts; you teach me wisdom in the inmost place" (Ps. 51:6).

Ask God to Help—God really does despise deceit because it is so dangerous and harmful. No matter what age you are, God wants to help you develop a habit of truthfulness. Pray this prayer as you ask God to help you move in that direction: *"God of all truth, I need your help. Because I want to be like you, I know that I must learn to love truth, but sometimes I don't know how. Lord, would you help me speak truth, believe it, and walk in it? Lord, help me catch myself when I start to lie or when I'm willing to let some form of deception operate in or through my life. Teach me to value truth as much as you do. In your name I pray, Jesus. Amen."*

addicted
to attention

Michelle was vain. Although she'd never say that she was more important, intelligent, or attractive than the rest of the girls in the church, some things are communicated without words. She was convinced that everyone loved her as much as she loved herself, and she treated others as if they were there to serve her needs, hang on her words, and applaud her every move.

Because she attended a small church, her social life was built around the dozen or so students in her youth group. And when they gathered together, Michelle dominated. She used sickeningly sweet laughter to get the attention of the boys she liked and rude and negative comments to destroy the ones she didn't. The girls were all scared of her because she was rarely nice to them. Instead, she picked on their fashion sense, put down their hairstyles, and made fun of their makeup, all the while flaunting her money in front of them.

Although they put up with her, her peers didn't enjoy her company. She thought the world revolved around her, and every day, every relationship was an opportunity to prove her superiority.

Bart was an egomaniac, and although everyone knew it, they liked him anyway. His obvious attempts to steal every conversation and turn it into his personal stage were entertaining, so his peers were willing to overlook his attention addiction for a season. However, his deeper relationships suffered as those closest to him began to recognize his tendencies.

Bart was a spotlight junkie, and he would do whatever was necessary to keep it shining brightly on him. He fabricated stories on a regular basis, because in his mind the merits of his life weren't strong enough to hold everyone's gaze. He used extreme flattery to win over the females in his life, and he always had a girlfriend. But because his ego demanded that he play the part of the knight in shining armor to every young lady, his dating relationships self-destructed as his affections wandered.

Although the adults in his life were quick to notice his motivations and habits, he refused to face the facts. His masks became things of legend as he lost all credibility and his lies were exposed.

As a young man growing up with a foundation of faith, a solid church experience, and a family that encouraged spiritual growth, you'd think that he would have understood that his direction was both destructive and unbiblical. However, he is still caught in the same trap. He continues to play the same games as he aimlessly wanders through life looking for the approval of others. He ambles through each year still seeking the spotlight and the respect of those around him. The only problem is that the people he wants to think well of him see right through his charade.

Sometimes girls can be too cute for their own good. That is definitely the case with Angie. Ever since she was very young, she has received compliments based on her appearance, and it has affected her in a negative way. She's decided that if she wants people to notice her, she must work to hide her imperfections and flaunt her good qualities.

Her makeup is aggressive, and her clothing is immodest. The tops are tight and the pants are low cut. Little is left to the imagination. Mothers turn and look away whenever she comes around, but the young men are fixated.

Her mannerisms are shallow and cliché. She giggles unnaturally whenever the boys start a conversation with her, and she goes fishing for compliments as she tries to get them to flirt back.

Even if you looked at only her eyes, you could see that she's longing for attention. Whenever she walks into a room, she scans it to find the attractive people and silently begs for their approval.

She's not a bad kid. She loves God, but her need to be noticed creates problems both for her and for those around her. Her refusal to be ignored is a testament to her vanity.

RECOGNIZE THE DROPS

Vanity is egotism that expresses itself primarily by craving attention. It goes on a rampage during the teenage years. High schools are filled with girls who are working to get everyone's attention and guys who are strutting their stuff. Vanity is on parade in the malls, the media, and everyday life. It even spills over into churches. Although Christians are supposed to be different, many times they get caught up in the same petty games and shallow charades.

Vanity reveals itself in many different ways. As you read through the following list, don't examine the people in your life to discover if they deal with it; rather, take an inventory of your own heart. Search for signs of this paralyzing attitude in your life. As you will discover, vanity will expend great amounts of energy trying to ignore a person's own flaws by pointing out the flaws of others. Don't fall for this trap. Instead, look closely at your own life and let the Lord speak to you about the unhealthy attitudes that might be hiding somewhere deep down inside.

ways vanity expresses itself

Flaunting possessions, abilities, and accomplishments. People who want attention will use this trick. They'll showcase their cars, cash, clothes, and homes, trying to impress. They'll build their personal definitions around the things they do well. Whether they use their athletic abilities, their musical expertise, or their scholastic achievements to point out their dominance, you can be sure they'll feature at least one thing in their always visible résumé of superiority.

If God has blessed you with material possessions or if he has given you unique abilities, you should be thankful. You shouldn't try to hide them from the world; however, they shouldn't define you either. So be yourself. Fight the urge to parade your blessings in front of others. Instead, live honestly, authentically, and humbly. Don't let those things go to your head or become the things you want everyone to notice about you.

Fishing for compliments. "Do you really think I'm pretty?" "How did I play?" Honest questions aren't the problem; motive is the real issue here. Some people bait the hook and go looking for positive comments. Some have even mastered the skill of negative remarks to receive desired praise. "I hate my hair" or "I wish I had your body" are statements that usually result in affirmative remarks.

If your insecurities drive you to go looking for verbal affirmation from others, recognize it and change it. If you're always searching for compliments, you're trying to use every relationship to your benefit. When you do this, you don't serve others or benefit them; you're only looking to get something from them. That's why you must refuse to play these silly games. Instead, work to find security in your relationship with the Lord. And look to invest more into every relationship than you will ever be able to get back.

Laboring for attention. Some people continually strive to be the center of attention. If they're not in the spotlight, they add either volume, humor, or other personal investments to draw the attention back to themselves.

Others will use their emotions to be noticed. These people have learned that a look of sadness and depression can guilt people into hovering and trying to cure what ails them. Vain people aren't content unless they are the center of attention and they are either dominating the conversation or are the topic being discussed.

John the Baptist declared that he wanted to drift out of the spotlight so that Jesus could steal the show (see John 3:30), and that should be our desire as well. However, the part of us that wants to be noticed, revered, and respected fights against that. These tendencies don't come from the spiritual part of us. Rather, they come from the part that is fleshly and selfish. That's why we must fight against them.

Rude and hurtful comments. By humiliating others and pointing out their faults, some people can achieve some level of evil satisfaction as they vault themselves above others. Sometimes these actions are motivated by contempt for the unpopular people who are "beneath" them. At other times they're inspired by jealousy.

The benefit of this habit is twofold. The first advantage is stated above—by pointing out others' faults, people can make themselves look better. The second is more subtle. By wielding negative opinions, a person who is looking for attention can demand it. Sure, some people will be either afraid of them or embittered by them, but these emotions are better than some of the alternatives. Although they aren't receiving the adulation of these people, at least they aren't being ignored.

Without a doubt, God wants us to love others and encourage them. Yet many Christians in our society have no problem tearing at others' esteem because they are different in some way. This is where we get to choose to submit to God's ways and his will as we reject the opportunity to lash out at others.

Exterior Dressings. As vanity runs rampant in our society, it may be more visible in the styles and fashions of the day than in any other way. Young ladies craving affection will settle for the attention inappropriate clothing can attract. Young men who long for love will be satisfied as long as they are noticed. A subculture of people who hate to be ignored will use body art as they scream for recognition.

I'm not suggesting that fashionable clothes are wrong. Nor am I recommending that people strive to conform to the style of their parents' generation. I'm simply proposing that some people, instead of enjoying the latest fads, use them as a tool to get attention. Again, motive is the key here. If you model your appearance in a way that demands that everyone notice you, then you are struggling with vanity.

reasons people struggle with vanity

Insecurity. Many obviously vain people come across as having it all together and having absolutely no problems. The truth is they're dominated by insecurities. The reason they work so hard to look perfect is that they don't like the way they look. They flaunt their past achievements because they're afraid that's all that makes them significant. And they ambush people with insults, giving the impression that they don't like them, because they really don't like themselves.

What is ironic about this entire process is that although they love for people to notice them and they long for attention, they don't want to really be discovered. They don't want anyone to see behind their mask into their fears and failures. And they don't want to expose their emotional state, their social instability, or the reality of their spiritual struggles.

The foundations of intense insecurity are too numerous to mention here, but God wants us to be free from this paralyzing view of ourselves. We are God's workmanship (Eph. 2:10), and he loves us. He continually whispers words of affirmation and comfort into our lives, but when we choose to fixate on our imperfections, we struggle to hear his expressions of love. To do away with insecurity, we must find ourselves in Christ and his view of us.

We live by other people's opinions. Something inside us cries out for approval. The only thing worse than having someone catch us doing something that portrays us as stupid, ugly, or clumsy is not being noticed at all. It is this fear of being ignored that forces so many people to clamor for others' applause and attention.

If our motivation is to impress the people around us, then our convictions are on shaky ground. Who we are, how we act, and what we value will shift depending on the people around us. If we long for the affirmation of other people, we will pattern our lives and develop our tastes around what society says is acceptable.

We are shallow. The majority of people in our society are not very deep. They value appearance and protect their image above all else. Those who are vain have adopted their systems and measures.

Rather than focusing on inner beauty and strength of character, we protect the comfort of our lives by keeping everything on a superficial level. We don't invest nearly as much time and energy into developing who we are as what we look like and what people think of us. Deep things take work to improve, but shallow things take little investment.

Learn God's Approach

God's plan was never that we be so self-absorbed that we forget about him or neglect the people around us. And he never wanted us to define our lives or find our confidence from other people. Therefore, he has some opinions and counsel on the area of vanity. Let's take a look at what he has to say.

"For by the grace given me I say to every one of you: Do not think of yourself more highly than you ought, but rather think of yourself with sober judgment, in accordance with the measure of faith God has given you" (Rom. 12:3). God's command is that we not think of ourselves too highly. My conviction is that this means we shouldn't be prideful, but it could also mean that we're not supposed to think of ourselves more often than we should. When we spend large chunks of time dwelling on nothing but self, we neglect our relationship with God and the other relationships we're supposed to invest in.

"Live in harmony with one another. Do not be proud, but be willing to associate with people of low position. Do not be conceited" (Rom. 12:16). We're supposed to live in unity and walk humbly with those around us, not taking into account how they measure up to our standards or how they benefit our status. Conceit and vanity demolish our desire and ability to walk with people as God wants us to.

"We do not dare to classify or compare ourselves with some who commend themselves. When they measure themselves by themselves and compare themselves with themselves, they are not wise" (2 Cor. 10:12). We're valuable because God loves us, created us for a purpose, and purchased us for a great price. But when we compare ourselves with others, trying to see how we measure up so we can determine our value, we add new components to the equation. In the end, this proves to be dangerous and destructive.

"Do nothing out of selfish ambition or vain conceit, but in humility consider others better than yourselves" (Phil. 2:3). *Nothing* is to be done selfishly or with vanity as our motivator. We are not to build any relationship with those goals in mind. We're not seeking a pecking order of life. We should consider others better, and we are to serve them.

"I also want women to dress modestly, with decency and propriety" (1 Tim. 2:9). What is modesty? What is decent dress? Those are issues you're going to have to wrestle with for yourself. But I would suggest that any article of clothing that teases those around you, playing on their lust and immorality, should be avoided. With your style, you should work to protect people around you who might struggle with those issues.

IT'S TIME TO CLIMB

Is there anyone who doesn't deal with insecurities? Nobody I've met.

Are there people out there who have reached a point in their spiritual lives where they don't care what others think? Very few!

On some level, you'll probably deal with these issues your entire life, but that doesn't mean you have permission to ignore them. Although you may never achieve perfection, by going in the right direction you can win some battles and gain back some ground. Just because you won't completely overcome vanity doesn't mean that you should let it run its course. By changing your perspectives, praying aggressive prayers, and refusing to live by the world's standards, you'll see God begin to transform this area of your life.

Here are a few practical suggestions to get you moving in the right direction:

Change your belief system. Belief systems fuel the insecurities in people's lives. We become convinced that we aren't attractive or thin enough, because we adopt the world's definition of beauty. We assume that we aren't valuable, because the school's testing system says we're below average. We must be worthless, because we don't have enough money, aren't athletic, or don't have the right friends. You see, these are all wrong belief systems that ignite our anxiety and send us searching for significance.

God's answer to our silent cries is not to help us measure up to the bogus standards, but rather to change our belief systems. He already has a standard, and you measure up very well. According to his system, you are not a mistake. You are not missing some gift that God forgot to place in your skill set. You were strategically and wonderfully made. You are God's masterpiece, the crown of his creation. And you are loved.

Those are the things you must begin to believe. You have to adopt those principles and let them change the way you think about yourself and the way you operate. To do that, you'll have to begin to meditate on those things.

The world advertises and propagates its belief system. You began to believe it simply because it's impossible to ignore. It has saturated the market and invaded your view. It has become embedded in your brain because you've heard it for so long, thought about it so often, and modified your behavior around it.

You must fight back with truth. Because you'll never be able to remove the influence of the world's system from your society, you must balance it with God's truth. You can begin by learning what God thinks about you, what he has put in you, and how he loves you. Then you memorize Scripture that speaks of God's provision and plan. And if you really want to get crazy, you can print out these thoughts and post them in your house and car. By putting them in places where you'll see them regularly, you're centering your new belief system around God and his Word.

With each grain of truth that you invest in your life, you change your belief system.

Don't try so hard. Here's a tip: Don't do anything to try to get attention. When you realize that you're interjecting a story because you want everyone to look at you, stop. If you start to dress a certain way because you know you can get people of the opposite gender to notice, change clothes. When you catch yourself putting someone down to get a laugh or showcase your wit, say something kind instead.

If you refuse to dominate conversations, run to the spotlight, and use your little tricks to get people's attention, then you're beginning to win this battle. It takes strong convictions mixed with steady discipline to operate in pure motives. If you're willing to put in the effort, your character will grow stronger and your addiction to the spotlight will become weaker.

Redirect the attention. One of the best ways to attack your need to be noticed is to point the attention toward someone else. Under your old way of operating, you would beg for the floor in a social situation. If you want to change that, you should begin to purposefully look for ways to redirect others until they begin to see and appreciate someone besides you.

Instead of hogging the stage, try offering a sincere compliment to someone else in the room. "You know what I appreciate about you, Jen? You are such a loyal friend." A comment like that will take the focus off of you and hand it to Jen. It will encourage and validate her in ways you could never imagine.

Why would you want to do that? The answer is simple. Because self is always at the center of vanity, you can overcome it only as you make others your priority. By redirecting the attention to someone else, you're ignoring your selfish needs and intentionally putting others first.

Reevaluate your style. I've been in full-time youth ministry for over fifteen years. And during that time I saw girls who struggled with the concept of modesty, and I wished to steer them in the right direction. As I saw young ladies (beautiful girls) show up to church events, youth trips, and camps in clothing that seemed to be missing some fabric, I searched for the all-encompassing Scripture that would give me some black-and-white material to back up my expectations. But I found none.

About seven years ago my battle intensified when my first daughter was born. From the very first moment I held her in my arms, I could picture her as a teenager. And I was scared. I now have two daughters, and because they both continue to look more and more like their mother every year, I know that my babies are going to be major babes.

As a father, I have two conflicting goals. The first is that I want Miranda and Courtney to be safe and protected. I don't want anyone taking advantage of them, using them, manipulating them, or picking up wrong signals from them. The second goal I have is to release my girls to grow up as individuals who can express themselves as Christian young women without the boundaries of legalism.

Now, don't get me wrong, there are rules in my house and there will continue to be as they age, but I'm battling with the issue of fashion versus modesty. I know that my girls will want to be fashionable, but I also want them to be modest. And unfortunately, in today's society, most of what is fashionable is not modest. I'm preparing for the day when I get to assist my daughters in making proper choices about what they wear and how they present themselves (thank God for my wife). I don't want them to attract the wrong kind of attention from the opposite sex, and I don't want them to feel the need to beg for attention with their appearance. But I do want them to feel stylish.

All of that to say that I don't take this topic lightly. I've given it much thought and prayer. And I will continue to give it more as the years come and go. But for now, let me share with you a thought I believe will protect you and those around you:

Flaunt your inner substance, not your appearance. Many people leave nothing to the imagination when it comes to the way that they dress. Women wear shirts that are cut both low and high. And pants that barely cover the parts that need covering. Add into that equation the tightness of the clothing or the see-through material, and there are problems.

On the other hand, certain guys love to take off their shirts and wear their pants low. Not because it's hot outside, but because they think they are.

Now, I realize you might want to argue with me (trust me, I've had a few conversations about this with some of my favorite students), but I'm convinced that Christians who long to be godly will shy away from ultra-revealing clothing.

What I really appreciate is when I see a young lady who is attractive but not exhibiting every physical feature. Rather, what is visible is her sincerity, humility, and tenderness.

I'm also grateful when I see young men who you know are hot properties to the women around them, but they aren't cocky. Instead, they exhibit a gentle spirit; an authentic, caring heart; and a spiritual hunger.

People like this have chosen to focus on the content instead of flaunting the package.

VIEW FROM THE TOP

The teenage years are filled with the temptation to beg for attention so you can build your reputation. Fight the urge. Don't play those games. Instead, keep your heart focused on Christ and continue pursuing him. One day the things you thought made you important will be exposed as a myth, but the person who walks closely with the Lord will never be disappointed.

GAINING GROUND

Ask Yourself This — Do you crave attention? How do you go after it most frequently? Do you recognize that this is dangerous and will get you into trouble? Using the list in this chapter, can you pinpoint a specific reason that you long to be noticed? Is there a way that you can begin to personally attend to this need instead of looking elsewhere for it to be met? What are some ways you can reaffirm God's love in your life? Was there one particular thing in this chapter that spoke to you? What are you going to do about it?

Key Scripture—"Do nothing out of selfish ambition or vain conceit, but in humility consider others better than yourselves" (Phil. 2:3).

Ask God to Help—If you have a problem with vanity, ego, or pride, you definitely need God's help. Without it, you'll continue to go in circles, spinning out of control. But with his help, you can begin to balance these areas of your life. You can begin by praying this prayer: *"Lord, you think I'm valuable. I know that, and that should be enough. But for some reason, I crave the attention, appreciation, and applause of others. Lord, would you help me see myself as you see me? Would you help me have a proper perspective on life so I'm not consumed with the need to perform or wear masks so others will notice me? I know that the symptoms point to the fact that I have a crisis of belief deep down inside me. Would you go down there and heal what needs to be healed and bring peace to those parts of my life? Thank you, Lord. In the name of Jesus, the one who loves me perfectly, I pray. Amen."*

3

all authority?

Growing up, I really wanted to be the person God wanted me to be. I wanted to live a life that was free from impurities and immorality. I knew I needed to protect myself from certain influences that would attack my character and eventually make my heart grow cold and callused, and I recognized that I wanted my life to count for Christ.

I wanted to be an upstanding Christian, so I knew I had to love the unlovely and fight for the outcast. I knew I needed to be respectful to adults and loyal to my friends. I chose to be a good example to the people around me, and I vowed not to put the girls I dated into dangerous situations. I had a lot of the details of Christianity figured out early, but I struggled with a couple of things. I learned to battle through some of them when I was a teenager, but there was one issue I ignored until I was an adult, and it caused me pain and affected many areas of my life.

The issue escaped my radar as a young man because I didn't see it as a major concern. I didn't think it was all that important. But it proved to be an obstacle I had to overcome. The issue was submission, and it revealed itself through the authority in my life.

Most of the authority figures in my life up to that point had experienced some of my disrespect. I'd lashed out at teachers who assigned homework that I considered busywork or taught subjects that I thought were irrelevant. I'd slandered a youth pastor who had skipped a prayer meeting or acted unjustly toward one of my friends. At work I'd cut corners when cleaning because I didn't have the integrity to do my job well. I'd disrespected my parents as well.

This disrespect and lack of submission wasn't an occasional occurrence; it was a habitual trend. There were a few leaders I agreed with, admired, and respected. These people didn't receive my negative behavior. But all those who didn't live up to my standards were targets, and they became victims.

My inclination toward disobedience didn't end as I graduated from high school and moved into college. As a matter of fact, my opinions became stronger, and my rebelliousness intensified with age. As my ministry began, I struggled. The first few pastors I worked for couldn't live up to my standards, so I found it easy to miss the mark of their expectations.

I don't remember when it happened, but I know where I was when it did. God began to convict me about my attitude toward my current employer. After several years of ministering under my pastor (I still attend his church), I began to show him disrespect. Because we were so similar in passion, temperament, and personality, we began to clash. Over a period of time, I began to question his vision, leadership, and gifts. My pride convinced me that I knew better than he did and that in many ways I was more effective in ministry than he was. The cycle was beginning to repeat itself. I felt justified in my judgments because our opinions were so different.

Over a period of time, I began to wake to the realization that my attitude and my actions were completely wrong. God began to walk me through Scripture as he convinced me that I had to submit and learn to support my pastor.

With great effort, I began to work toward that end. Rather than jab at him with a sarcastic comment intended to point out one of his flaws, I began trying to build him up, encourage him, and let him know I was on his side. Instead of talking negatively about him, I began to pray for him, asking God to continue to shape him and mold him. Instead of doing my own thing, I discovered his vision, and I worked to help him achieve it.

I won't lie to you. It was hard. At first I didn't enjoy it, but then I began to realize that through the whole process I was being refined as well. I had adopted one of God's commands, and by working to implement it, I was becoming more like Christ.

There were two other benefits. The first is that my pastor and I became closer and our relationship became stronger. The second is that as I learned this lesson and began to live it, God promoted me into a different and more fulfilling ministry. It was as if there was a load of potential hidden behind a wall. I'd been trying to unlock it, but something was holding it back. As soon as I realized that I had a responsibility to submit to those over me and I began to work toward that end, it was as if the wall broke and I stepped into a new season of my life. A good season.

RECOGNIZE THE DROPS

Something inside us hates submission. Because we are selfish and controlling, we despise the idea that another person could be in a position of authority over us. Some people struggle to give complete lordship to Christ because they can't allow God to be in authority over them.

Make no mistake about it: God's desire for us is that we walk under the proper umbrella of authority. It is commanded, and there are many benefits that accompany proper submission. There are very few good reasons to ever disobey those who are in authority over you. Whether they are your teachers, parents, boss, or spiritual leaders, God makes it clear that we are to always walk in obedience and submission.

However, many people have issues with applying this order. And defiance is expressed in many ways. Here are a few of the ways that people have avoided submission and the reasons so many struggle with it. As you will notice, there is a direct correlation between the way someone responds to their authorities on earth and the way they respond to the authority in heaven.

ways people respond incorrectly to authority

Blatant disobedience. One of the clearest signs that someone is refusing to walk in proper submission to authority is blatant disobedience. Outright defiance and stubborn refusal to conform to the wishes of those above you is nothing other than rebellion, and it can be seen in the relationships of parents and teens, teachers and students, employers and employees, and every other known relationship where authority and submission play a part.

This can even be seen in God's relationships with some of his kids. Although his children know a mandate has been given, many refuse to submit to his plan of action. "Walk in purity" is one expectation, and although it is understood, it is many times ignored. "Love the person everyone else makes fun of" is another, yet it also is disregarded.

God expects us to obey his commands, yet many times we refuse. How can we say we are followers of Christ unless we choose to allow him to guide and direct us with his commands, statutes, and laws?

Partial obedience. In order to give the impression that they are in compliance with the authority figure in their life, some people will obey but not completely. By cutting corners and working only halfheartedly, they can do enough to get by without completely serving the one above them. Instead of really cleaning their rooms when asked, some children clear the mess by shoving things in closets and under beds. However, they haven't obeyed the intent of the parent's request. Employees will cut out of work early if it can go unnoticed or ignore a need, assuming that the first person to acknowledge it will be the one who has to meet it. Instead of doing their homework, many students get together before class to share answers. This gives the impression that they're obeying the teacher and completing the work; however, it is an example of partial obedience.

Are there people who give only partial obedience to God? There absolutely are — those Christians who choose which parts of his commands don't infringe too much upon the lifestyle they seek while refusing to acknowledge the ones that are difficult to obey.

God is looking for complete obedience from us. He wants us to obey the intent of his commands, not only the actual requirement. When we pick and choose what to obey while consciously ignoring the conviction of the Holy Spirit and the Word of God, we are undermining his authority. Make no mistake, when it comes to God, partial obedience is complete disobedience.

Talking back. Although it is very common for people who are living for themselves, making no attempt to live for Christ or acknowledge him in their lives, I'm convinced that it grieves God's heart when he hears Christians talking back to authority. Teachers and principals get it all the time, as do the majority of parents in this nation. Brilliant and well-mannered children who are examples of godliness in so many areas of their lives transform into little rebels with an aggressive and defiant streak when they disagree with those in positions of authority. It isn't right. Those in authority deserve better, and God expects more.

Although I haven't actually seen or heard anyone talking back to God, I understand it happens all the time. People who disagree with God's decisions or the direction he is leading will defiantly posture themselves against his will as if they were arguing with him. "God, I will not break up with my girlfriend." Or "I don't want to be a pastor." They may not shout the words, but by choosing their will over God's, in essence they are talking back.

Again, although it's contrary to our human nature, God's desire for us is that we submit to the authorities he has put into our lives. And when we argue with him or refuse to obey him, we reveal that we value our opinion more than his.

Talking bad. The whispers can be heard in churches, offices, and schools all over the world. Humanity has decided that it is our right and obligation to point out the faults of those in authority over us. Many have no regard for the people God has put into authority, as they have decided they must share their opinions and observations with anyone who will listen.

Let me be blunt. This isn't right. Although there will never be a human being who will sit in any kind of authority position who will be perfect in their decisions, character, or philosophies, God doesn't give us permission to attack them or talk behind their back. When we do, we are operating in the schemes of the enemy, who works to bring confrontation through accusation.

But God operates through love expressed through encouragement and corporate unity.

reasons people respond incorrectly to authority

Pride. Some people's pride demands that they be right and all others be wrong. They refuse to submit because in doing so, they're admitting that the person above them is actually superior.

It's amazing to me how human beings can hold on to their opinions and think that they're superior to everyone else's. For example, a young child can debate with several adults about an issue, because their pride has convinced them that their position is right and all the others are wrong.

It is no secret that God condemns our pride (see 1 Peter 5:5), so we must work to overcome it. God's desire for us in the area of authority is that we choose to submit to the wishes of those in leadership over us even if it steps on our pride. Actually, as God tries to weed pride out of our lives, one of the tools he uses is the people in authority over us.

Laziness. Usually those over us expect more of us than we require of ourselves. They want us to do our homework, complete the projects they have given us, do our chores, or live responsibly. Many times this infringes upon our laziness. We would rather do as little as possible, and that's one of the reasons we refuse to submit to them.

This can be seen in the spiritual realm as well. God (many times using our spiritual leaders to encourage us in this direction) wants us to pursue holiness and servanthood, all the while aspiring to become more like him. This takes work. That's why many Christians refuse to submit to God and become dissatisfied with their spiritual leaders. Their pastors advocate a lifestyle that takes intentional effort, and rather than hear the voice of the

Lord in the challenge of these leaders, they leave the church looking for a more comfortable environment.

If you're going to walk with Christ, you'd better come to grips with the fact that God does have requirements and expectations. The lazy Christian will not grow, nor will he be satisfied. The lazy Christian ultimately will be miserable.

Selfishness. Like little children, sometimes we clamor for our way. We like our lives, our rules, and our philosophies. We hold on to our rights as if they were the most precious things in the world. Selfishly we fight for our comfort and convenience. If anyone comes into our lives who might try to infringe upon our choices, we bite and scratch, debate and argue. Defiantly we protest, "You can't tell me what to do."

And as you already know, whenever you submit to authority, you're saying, "I choose to please you. I put your priorities over my own and your goals above my objectives." This grates against our selfish nature.

As we grow with God, one of our ultimate goals is to become less self-centered and more Christ-centered. Instead of becoming absorbed in our desires, we begin to see the big picture of God's desire, both for us and for the world.

Dealing with authority is an issue many people struggle with. Not only are many directly defying God's mandate, but they're causing themselves problems. The rewards for submitting to and serving those in leadership positions are numerous (favor, promotion, kindness, trust, and so forth), but people who are desperately trying to discover these benefits through manipulation, dishonesty, and trickery are continually frustrated.

God honors those who respect, esteem, and serve those in leadership. And until we figure out that God's ways are better than ours, we'll continue to hit the wall. But on the other hand, as we learn to submit and walk justly before our superiors, we'll discover God's blessings in so many ways.

Learn God's Approach

The idea of authority comes directly from God. He is our leader, and we are called to submit to him. As Christians, we are required to choose his ways over our plans.

Submission is a central theme in the Bible, and it's an important and foundational philosophy in the Christian walk. It starts at the top; we must first submit to God. However, it must go deeper than that. As men and women of God, we must also choose to relinquish control to all the other authorities in our lives. It is biblical and it is a mandate. Take a look at the strong language used in Scripture whenever leadership and authority are discussed.

> "He said to his men, 'The LORD forbid that I should do such a thing to my master, the LORD's anointed, or lift my hand against him; for he is the anointed of the LORD'" (1 Sam. 24:6). David knew that even an evil king is placed in that position by the Lord himself. And even though King Saul was trying to kill the young shepherd, he knew he should not and could not retaliate. Wouldn't it be great if the Christians in the world today understood this principle and, instead of taking it upon themselves to point out their leaders' faults, refused to "touch" them in any negative way?

> "But David said to Abishai, 'Don't destroy him! Who can lay a hand on the LORD's anointed and be guiltless?'" (1 Sam. 26:9). The man after God's own heart (Acts 13:22) knew the priority that God put on authority issues. Even though it looked as if God had given the king into his hands to

kill, David knew that Saul was better left up to God. He refused to attack.

"Everyone must submit himself to the governing authorities, for there is no authority except that which God has established. The authorities that exist have been established by God. Consequently, he who rebels against the authority is rebelling against what God has instituted, and those who do so will bring judgment on themselves" (Rom. 13:1–2). It's hard to escape the wording here. If you believe that every word of the Bible is inspired by God (as I do), then you have to notice that it talks about all authorities as being God's idea. Not some, but all. And it says outright that those who rebel against these authorities will bring judgment upon themselves. Think about that the next time you want to argue with a teacher or whisper a comment about an authority figure.

"I urge, then, first of all, that requests, prayers, intercession and thanksgiving be made for everyone—for kings and all those in authority, that we may live peaceful and quiet lives in all godliness and holiness. This is good, and pleases God our Savior" (1 Tim. 2:1–3). Not only are we to submit to those in authority, but we are to pray for them as well. This pleases God. What more inspiration to pray for them do we need?

"Obey your leaders and submit to their authority. They keep watch over you as men who must give an account. Obey them so that their work will be a joy, not a burden, for that would be of no advantage to you" (Heb. 13:17). Obedience is commanded. And not simply to the point where we consent enough not to irritate authority figures, but to the point where we are a joy to those above us. To do this, we must go out of our way to support them, encourage them, and demonstrate God's love to them.

IT'S TIME TO CLIMB

Okay, so we know God wants us to submit to and support authority, but it doesn't come naturally to us. As a matter of fact, many times it defies logic and proves to be the exact opposite of what we want to do. This being the case, how do we move in the right direction? Like most things in our spiritual lives, dealing with authority properly takes a lot of discipline, and it requires a conscious choice. When we're convinced that this is God's expectation of us and we're committed to making it happen, God will work with us to make sure we're moving in the right direction.

To make this work, we must have an intentional and strategic plan. Here are some things you can begin to do as you adopt this principle into your life:

1. *Submit in your heart.* To deal properly with authority, you're going to have to submit to it. This isn't just an outward submission; it begins in the heart. With God's help (note that you may need to ask God to help you accomplish this), you can submit to authority even if you dislike or disagree with some of the authority figures in your life.

If you're dealing with a teacher or employer who really gets you going, you may need to consciously surrender your rights and choose to obey their requests while refusing to get angry with them. Making this decision in your car or in the hall before you encounter them is always wise.

If you recognize that you really struggle in this area of submission, you may need to incorporate this principle into your prayer life. "*Lord, help me submit to that person. From my heart, I choose to obey, comply, and support them. Thank you for helping me with this, Lord.*"

2. *Pray for those over you.* As we have already discussed, God commands us to pray for those over us (see 1 Tim. 2:2), but there's

another element at work here as well. When we pray for them, not only are we obeying a command, but we're also changing our hearts. It's impossible to consistently pray for someone and not begin to care about them on some level. If we genuinely ask God to give them wisdom to accomplish their responsibilities and give them favor so that they will be blessed, a fondness for them will grow in our hearts. It's impossible to invest in prayer for someone's life and remain angry, bitter, or distant from them.

3. *Guard your mouth.* You must watch what you say, especially when you're speaking about one of the authority figures God has put into your life. Although David's comments in 1 Samuel were about bringing physical harm to "the LORD'S anointed," I believe he was just as adamant about speaking negatively about the king. He knew that God was the ultimate and only judge; therefore, it wasn't his responsibility to point out the king's flaws.

As a Christian, you must not gossip, slander, or speak negatively about anyone. That goes double for those in authority. Guard your mouth. Clamp it down and don't let any of those negative, degrading, judgmental, or aggressive comments escape. And if they do, make them right. Ask for forgiveness from the one you spoke them to and the one you spoke them about.

4. *Work as unto the Lord.* Colossians 3:23 tells us that we are to work for the Lord, not for men. If we can adopt this attitude, everything will find a proper balance. When we aren't being watched, we might be tempted to cut corners. However, when we realize that God is always watching us, we won't try to get away with anything. If we're working for a person, how much we like that person or want their approval will determine the quality of our work. However, if we're working for the Lord, we're going to want to please him.

One other thing to consider is that everything we do has a larger part to play than we realize. Our attitude and our performance are a testimony to those around us. We serve a God of excellence, and we should want those around us to understand that. By doing our part, working hard, and doing the best we can, we'll communicate silently to those around us about the God we serve.

5. Adopt the philosophy of extreme obedience. In a world that's used to people giving only minimal effort, what would extreme obedience communicate to those over you? What if you went above and beyond their expectations? What if you took care of the need before anyone mentioned it to you? Do you think you would find the favor of your leaders? Do you think it would please the Lord?

At home, you could clean the kitchen before anyone asked. At work, you could personally take responsibility for the cleanliness of your area. Instead of hiding from obligation, you could ask for it. At school, you might not be the brightest student, but you could be the hardest working.

Not that you do it with these motives, but if and when you begin to work toward extreme obedience, you'll set an example for those around you, you'll catch the attention of those above you, and you'll ultimately please your heavenly authority.

Submission is a big deal to God. He wants us to learn to relinquish our rights as we work with and for those in leadership roles. His Word makes it clear. It's a command, not a request. Yet many Christians choose to ignore this principle, because it goes against what they've been taught. However, this is one of those issues where we simply must obey. It's time we begin to submit to the authorities in our lives even if we don't agree with them.

VIEW FROM THE TOP

As we have already stated, submission begins with the ultimate authority. So I ask you, Are you submitted to God? Have you surrendered to his leading, or are you still demanding your way? I strongly encourage you to pay careful attention to these questions. Make sure you can answer them honestly, and make sure you like the answers you've given.

GAINING GROUND

Ask Yourself This—Are there people in authority whom you struggle with? Do you have a tendency to rebel against what God has instituted? What does God think about that? What can you do to begin to walk in God's plan for submission? Do you think your attitude about submission has any connection to how you do or don't submit to God and his plans for your life?

Key Scripture—"Everyone must submit himself to the governing authorities, for there is no authority except that which God has established. The authorities that exist have been established by God. Consequently, he who rebels against the authority is rebelling against what God has instituted, and those who do so will bring judgment on themselves" (Rom. 13:1–2).

Ask God for Help—If you're like most of us, you've struggled to submit to authorities at different times in your life. If you realize that you need God's help in this, then pray this prayer: *"God, first of all, before anything else, I submit to you. You're not just my Savior, but you're my Lord. I want what you want for my life. On top of that, I need your help to submit to the earthly authorities in my life. God, you know how difficult it is for me to follow them. Could you help me with my attitude toward them? Show me how to submit in my heart. And teach me to work for you only. Lord, thank you for never giving up on me. I love you. Amen."*

part 2

explosive
emotions

4

overcoming anger

When I looked in the mirror, I saw five people standing in the aisle. I stopped the bus as soon as I realized a fight had broken out in back.

As I brought the vehicle to a stop along the freeway, I tried to both control and assess the situation. Two guys were holding Tim back, so I realized he must have lashed out at someone. I wasn't prepared to deal with the fact that the person he'd attacked was a girl.

All five of the people who were standing joined me outside. As they left the bus, Tim and Rachelle, who was half his size, were still jawing at one another as the others tried to keep them apart.

Once we got outside, I forbade Tim and Rachelle to speak and I asked the others what had happened. It turns out that she'd been teasing him about some family issues, when she finally found a hot spot. As soon as she mentioned mental instability, he jumped out of his seat and threw a solid right hook to her left eye. The mark was still visible.

Tim had grown up in a very unstable environment. His parents' marriage had never been solid, and at the time of that bus ride, his family was wading through a messy and painful divorce. His mom had spent some time in a psychiatric ward, and Tim had spent a month in one as well. When Rachelle, who was intentionally trying to provoke him, mentioned that, he lost control and went after her.

Tim began to cry from embarrassment, and I dismissed the three peacemakers and told them to get back on the bus. I didn't want Tim to be even more embarrassed by the shame that would come from having others see him lose control both physically and emotionally.

Now that it was just the three of us, I spoke to Rachelle first. Her spite and attitude were still apparent. I could tell she was proud that she'd successfully gotten to him. Although she apologized for her part in the outburst, she was not repentant. I decided it was better to send her back on the bus and talk with Tim.

With just the two of us out in the night air, we began to make progress. With no one else around, his emotions flowed freely as he told me how embarrassed he was that he'd lost control. He couldn't believe he'd let his anger boil over to the point that he actually hit a girl. And over forty of his peers saw him do it. He told me he had an anger problem, but he didn't know what to do about it. He confessed that he had little control and that this wasn't the first time he'd done something stupid. He told me it was the outburst itself that was most frustrating, not the things he'd gotten mad about in the first place.

His anger would flare up again and again until he learned to deal with it. This vicious cycle needed attention. It had gotten him into severe circumstances in the past (school suspensions, fistfights with friends, smudges on his reputation, and people being afraid of him). And if he didn't get it taken care of, the repercussions of the flare-ups would become more severe as he got older.

RECOGNIZE THE DROPS

Anger is a problem in our society, and it's a major issue among the younger generations. Anger occurs in varying levels, from minor irritation to violent rage. And it affects families, communities, and relationships in varying degrees, from mild anxiety to paralyzing fear.

Hate crimes have been linked to hidden anger that suddenly exploded onto the scene. Abuse situations have been linked to a parent's inability to correctly deal with anger. Students have abused teachers, and teenagers have attacked parents. Moms have physically assaulted children, and husbands have been violent with their wives. Aggressive and impulsive actions motivated by anger flow in every direction. The attackers lash out without respecting authority or taking time to evaluate consequences of their actions. Anger wounds innocent bystanders who don't understand what's happening as well as the people who have brought on the rage. And possibly one of the scariest things about anger is that it tends to wound even those who are loved the most.

To get a handle on anger, we must understand what its roots are and how it responds. Everyone is different, and there is no way one chapter can cover all the circumstances and story lines. The following information is an overview of some of the most common reasons and results of anger.

reasons for anger

Rejection. Although anger is triggered by a vast array of emotions and events, one of the most familiar sources is rejection.

When someone feels rejected by their family, their peers, or society in general, they take that sense of alienation and hide it away in their heart. If they don't uncover it and deal with it, it can incubate there until it becomes full-blown anger.

Because our society works hard to enhance our insecurities and isolate us from others, this hiding away of anger is a common theme in some people's lives. When anger is pushed down inside, the one who suffers will tend to lash out at untimely moments and overreact in different situations.

Embarrassment. If someone feels embarrassed, they might respond in a negative and volatile way. Rather than walking away with their head hung low like they did as a child, they might strike out without thinking through their actions.

Pain. The anguish of emotional distress can cause a person to act out in anger.

For example, one of my sutdents, whose name was Allen, told me about the divorce of his parents and the other difficult situations in his life as we tried to walk through his anger. For years he had been lying to himself, trying to live convinced that the divorce didn't affect him. But after yet another public outburst where he attacked a fellow student for no real reason, he realized that something inside was feeding his emotions and rage. The pain of the past several years was revealing itself in his destructive behavior. Allen finally realized why he was struggling to control his actions. The hidden aching in his heart was amplifying his uncontrolled emotions.

Fear. When someone is caught off guard by feelings of fear, it emphasizes lack of control and comes out as anger. Fear reminds the victim that they really have no power in their life, and this strong emotion manipulates them into actions with consequences.

the way anger reacts

Outbursts. The most common angry reaction is an explosion of one sort or another. On occasion it is an outburst of tears, other times it is a verbal assault, and other times it is a physical display. Whether there are fists flying, dangerous words soaring, or tears bursting onto the scene, these outbursts are never the way to deal with anger.

Withdrawal. Let me reemphasize that everyone is different and therefore deals differently with anger. While some run after people to take care of it once and for all, others back away completely. By intentionally isolating themselves from people, they feel they are doing the right thing, when many times this kind of hiding is actually preparing them for a holocaust of emotion. At the time, withdrawing may look like the more mature way to deal with a situation when someone angers you, but many times it's more dangerous. Running from your anger won't make it go away. You must discover how to deal with it appropriately.

Sarcasm. Some lash out physically, others verbally. I have met many people who deal with their anger by laying out land mines of sarcasm. These bombs, although the person says "I was just teasing," are laced with bitterness and unforgiveness. In the hands of a skilled and witty person, sarcasm is a more dangerous weapon than anything that might be used in a physical attack.

Attacking a substitute. Sure young people feel rejected at school, but it's their parents who get yelled at and it's their siblings who get doors slammed in their faces. Instead of reacting at school, they come home and attack a substitute. Fathers do this when they take the tension of their jobs out on their families. Mothers do it when they rain unhappiness and resentment on their husbands and children because they can't find a way to take it out on the part of life that is sucking the joy out of them.

Escaping through a substitute. Some people use addictions to forget their anxiety. Drugs, alcohol, and food have all been used. Some get caught up in the fairy-tale world of entertainment so they don't have to concentrate on the anger-inducing realities of their real lives. Others run to temporary relationships that make them smile to avoid the ones that frustrate them.

Many people are slaves to their anger. They wander through life wondering when the next bomb will go off and what the damage will be. Some tiptoe around loved ones, silently praying that their anger won't wound their relationship yet not convinced that they have the restraint to control it.

Anger is a problem. It has many roots, and it expresses itself in many ways. All are dangerous and all have consequences. But anger is an issue that God can help anyone overcome.

LEARN GOD'S APPROACH

Anger is an issue God has spoken of many times in Scripture. The Bible gives us edicts to live by, and it gives us glimpses into the lives of people who let anger control their actions. Let's take a look at a couple of these verses.

"A gentle answer turns away wrath, but a harsh word stirs up anger" (Prov. 15:1). When someone approaches you with fury in their eyes, the best response is humble and gentle words. Don't stoke the fires. Although your emotions may begin to boil as well, choose wisely and bring peace with your words instead of feeding the turbulent mood.

"Anger is cruel and fury overwhelming, but who can stand before jealousy?" (Prov. 27:4). Anger is nasty, brutal, and dangerous. It wounds people and destroys relationships.

"A fool gives full vent to his anger, but a wise man keeps himself under control" (Prov. 29:11). Emotional maturity becomes visible in many ways. One of those is the way you handle your intense emotions. Control comes with practice, discipline, and willpower. The foolish person lashes out, but the wise man knows when and how to react when the feelings build up.

"Jesus entered the temple area and drove out all who were buying and selling there. He overturned the tables of the money changers and the benches of those selling doves" (Matt. 21:12). There is an anger that is righteous in nature. Most anger is seeded in selfish emotion because of inconvenience or personal discomfort; however, this kind of anger is aroused at injustice. When there is an unholy unrest in you because of the way God is being represented or mocked or because of the way his children are being treated, you might just be experiencing righteous indignation. You still need wisdom in how to respond in those moments, but God's Spirit could be pushing you toward some kind of reaction.

"'In your anger do not sin': Do not let the sun go down while you are angry, and do not give the devil a foothold" (Eph.

4:26–27). Is it a sin to let your emotions boil? No, it's human nature. However, it turns to sin as we react harshly or let the anger ferment. Once we recognize that we are becoming angry at someone's actions or ignorance, we must deal with it. Anger that is allowed to fester becomes a way for the enemy of our souls to enter into our lives and cause damage.

"Get rid of all bitterness, rage and anger, brawling and slander, along with every form of malice" (Eph. 4:31). Bottom line: God's command is that we get rid of anger and rage. We don't want it to wreak havoc in our lives.

"But now you must rid yourselves of all such things as these: anger, rage, malice, slander, and filthy language from your lips" (Col. 3:8). Again, there is no way around it: God's command is to get rid of all of it.

"My dear brothers, take note of this: Everyone should be quick to listen, slow to speak and slow to become angry, for man's anger does not bring about the righteous life that God desires" (James 1:19–20). Man's anger does not bring about a righteous life. If our desire and our goal is to become more Christ-like and to bring him glory, then we can't ignore this problem of anger.

IT'S TIME TO CLIMB

Many students who grew up in my youth ministry battled with anger. Some deal with it continually even as adults, but some have broken free. Now that they're married and have families of their own, some of their spouses are frightened by their random outbursts. However, there are some people whose spouses feel protected even though they're around someone who used to be emotionally turbulent. Why? Because they handed their problem to God and asked for his help.

If you deal with anger and you want to break free from your patterns, there is good news. You can change. You can learn to control your outbursts, and with time you can cultivate peace in your heart that will drive off the excessive anger that now resides there.

Here are a few steps that you can begin to take today to ensure that the people who mean the most to you won't have to wander around afraid of your next flare-up:

Recognize, acknowledge, and deal with issues that cause your anger. If you can discover the things that push your buttons, you can begin to get a handle on them. If you tend to go off when someone embarrasses you, you can see it coming from a mile away and you can make the necessary adjustments.

To do this, take time and write down the times that you have lost control of your anger in the past several weeks. If there have been several times, just write down the most severe occurrences. If your explosions are less frequent, make note of the most severe occasions you can remember.

After you write the situations down, evaluate the circumstances that led up to the outburst. Was there always one person involved? Was there a recurring theme in the conversation? Was there a particular mood that was prevalent?

Now using that list, systematically assess these incidents and take precautions so your anger doesn't expose itself again.

Pray and ask God to forgive you for lashing out. Although there are occasions (see Matt. 21:12) where reactions to anger are righteous, most are not. When a person loses control and aggressively speaks words that could wound, or they violently attack another, they have sinned. Whenever we cross that line, we need to ask God to forgive us and help us the next time we are in a similar situation.

Using the list you made earlier, comb through the situations and ask God to forgive you for each of those transgressions.

Pray for the person who provoked your anger. If you want to forgive the person who wronged you, and you truly want to gain control over your intense feelings toward them, you should pray for God's interaction in their life.

People sometimes harbor bitterness, waiting for the next opportunity to get back at someone who provoked their anger. However, this is never healthy. You need to give these offenses over to Christ and allow him to work the miracle of forgiveness in your heart. Although it is difficult, it is necessary. You can begin the process by simply praying for the person who provoked you.

"God, would you be with Sara? You know that sometimes we argue and she makes me mad, but I know you love her. And if she's going through tough times, would you be with her? Lord, let her know that you love her." A prayer like that will work miracles in both your lives.

If possible, find the root of your anger and deal with it. Although you may think it's your mom who is making you angry, could it be that she's just the substitute you're taking your anger out on? If you're abusing and disrespecting your dad, could it be that you're treating him poorly because something is falling apart in another area of your life?

By taking the time to examine your life, you just might uncover the painful issue that is truly agitating you. You might discover the real root that's affecting many areas of your life. If you can locate the source, you can address it. If you can alleviate the real problem, you might get a handle on some of your self-destructive tendencies.

If your anger is strong in the moment, try to calm down so you don't overreact. Stop! Slow down! Breathe! Count to ten! Leave the room! Whatever it takes, get perspective before you react. If you respond while you are still annoyed, most likely you'll say or do something you'll regret. But if you can remove the emotion (at least on some level), you can control the situation a little better.

If you sense that you're about to blow up at your parents, excuse yourself. Go to your room and get perspective. Pray. Ask for God's help and then return and have a rational conversation.

Don't react in your emotion, because the compassion and love that God commands you to walk in can't operate in your anger. By taking a few minutes to calm down, you might save yourself some embarrassment and spare another person some scars.

VIEW FROM THE TOP

Although some people give excuses for their outbursts ("It's genetic. My family has always been volatile."), there are no excuses God would accept. Some prefer to feel justified ("Did you see what he did to me?"), but there is no justification. God's ways are higher than ours, and he doesn't want us lashing out in our anger.

Unbridled anger is ugly, and it rips through families and friendships, leaving damaged people. However, people who are working to grow closer to God and honor him with their lives can overcome their tendencies.

GAINING GROUND

Ask Yourself This—Do you know anyone who has an anger problem? Have you ever been the victim of one of their explosions? Do you personally have a problem with anger? Have you ever lost control in front of a group in a way that embarrassed you later? Does that happen often? When was the last time it happened? Could you relate to any of the reasons for anger listed in this chapter? Which one? Was there one of the ways that anger reacts that you experience more often than the others? If you do struggle with anger, what steps are you going to take to control that emotion more?

Key Scripture— "A fool gives full vent to his anger, but a wise man keeps himself under control" (Prov. 29:11).

Ask God to Help—Anyone can develop stability in their emotional life and overcome an anger problem. If you need God's help with this, pray this prayer: *"God, I realize that anger is an ugly emotion. I don't like to see it slip out into my life. I don't like the way I think when I'm angry. I don't like the things I do, and I don't like what I say when I'm angry. So, Lord, I ask for your help. God, would you give me strength to overcome my anger? Would you help me notice my anger starting to rise up before it's at full boil? With your help I'll try and keep myself under control. Give me strength, dear Father. It's in the name of Jesus I pray. Amen."*

5

what to do when all hope is gone

When Sarah arrived at the church ready for camp, I was slightly surprised. She had never been very social. As a matter of fact, you could say she was a loner. Rarely did she attend youth services, and I couldn't remember the last time she'd been on a youth outing. We saw her on Sundays, when her parents insisted she join them at church, but other than that we didn't know her.

As we rode the bus out to the camp grounds, a couple of us tried to get to know her but were unsuccessful. Although we tried to involve her in conversations, she worked hard to stay out of them. She looked sullen and refused to look us in the eye. What I saw that day concerned me.

When we arrived at the camp and everyone was getting situated in their cabins, I pulled Ellen, one of my best youth leaders, aside and talked to her about Sarah. Ellen was great at breaking through walls, building friendships, and then using those bonds to minister to the deep parts of students' lives. I told her about my observations and concerns about Sarah, who was going to be in her cabin. I told her to do her thing. And that she did.

By the second day, you could see Sarah beginning to come out of her shell. Though she didn't smile much and her posture was constricted, she was entering into conversations around the meal table. By the third day, she seemed more spiritually interested. And by the fourth day, something was visibly breaking free in her life.

After four days of observing her, praying for her, and building a relationship, Ellen stepped in and went to work. Just after midnight, she started up a conversation with Sarah in the bathroom of their cabin. The talk had specific goals. Ellen wanted to know what was in Sarah's past so that she could encourage her and help her grow.

Because Ellen had heard many wild and crazy tales of abuse and neglect, she had braced herself for the worst. But she was surprised to discover that the haunting emotions that had filled Sarah's heart since she was ten weren't attached to anything in particular. Her parents were supportive and still married. She hadn't been abused, and there had been no dramatic changes or traumatic experiences.

Although she couldn't pinpoint any specific incident that sent her into a shell, she had withdrawn. She had been secluded in a pit of negative emotions and despair for the past five years, and she didn't know why.

Looking into her new friend's eyes, Sarah explained, "Ever since I can remember, I've been depressed. I feel stupid for feeling this way. I know that most of my friends have it much worse than me, so I feel guilty for being so sad all the time."

Ellen began to shed tears with Sarah as she spoke kind words and promised to pray until things changed. Shortly after that, they joined in prayer, shared an embrace, and then headed back to their bunks. For quite some time Ellen lay there praying for a miracle to take place in Sarah's life. Ellen lay on her sleeping bag, begging God to help Sarah overcome the emotions that had been so strong.

RECOGNIZE THE DROPS

Those who have never experienced deep depression might struggle to understand just how paralyzing it can be. But for those who have felt its attack, depression is a hated foe.

Depression can be defined as strong feelings of unhappiness and despair, and it affects people of all ages, races, classes, and genders. Sometimes it can be attributed to a situation or circumstance, such as the loss of a loved one, problems in the family, or a dramatic change in location or lifestyle. But there are other occasions when these strong feelings of hopelessness creep in, poisoning major areas of a person's life without any apparent reason.

In a recent study it was discovered that every year nearly 5 percent of all teenagers are identified as clinically depressed.[1] That's a huge number when you consider that those are just the ones who are identified as having a strong form of depression. If we added in the students who are never diagnosed or those who deal with depression in moderate amounts, that number would soar. Encompassed in that revised number would be high percentages of students who attend every school, are members of every church, and come from every possible background.

Here's a list of the reasons that depression creeps into people's lives and a list of the ways its effects can be seen.

reasons for depression

Chemical Imbalances. Although depression is thought of primarily as an emotional thing, on occasion the emotions are heightened and intensified by chemical imbalances. If a person is experiencing depression in a way that's completely unexplainable in other terms or extremely intense in its attack, they should consult a doctor to see if their body is out of balance.

Biological Factors. Physical factors can contribute to depression. Things like a lack of sleep, insufficient exercise, physical illness, and improper diet will heighten the sense of depression. When someone is dealing with depression, they should consider all these possible causes while trying to evaluate the cause and uncover a cure.

Rejection. Rejection by someone significant can send a person spiraling into the pit of despair.

Abuse. When a person is trying to wade through the memories and sift through the emotions that come with abuse, they may slump into a depression. How long that lasts can vary. It may be severe depression lasting for a long stretch or mild despair lasting only a short time.

Stress. High levels of stress can send the emotions on a roller coaster, resulting in bottom-out moments of depression.

Guilt. The burden of guilt can steal someone's joy, hope, and peace. And it can carry with it the consequence of depression. Depression is a common side effect for people who have made mistakes in the area of their sexual choices. The memories of their weaknesses are strong, continually reminding them of their failures. So in walks depression.

ways depression reacts

Physically. People dealing with depression have a tendency to be lethargic, lacking energy. Their sleep habits may be affected too—depressed people often don't want to ever get out of bed. Changes in appetite are normal as well.

Emotionally. It makes sense that depression, a disease of the emotions, will be expressed in emotional ways. Moodiness is common, with some people regularly breaking into tears at odd moments and for obscure reasons. And depressed people struggle to hide their sadness from those around them as their posture, expression, and eyes declare their mood.

Short attention span. People struggling with depression have problems concentrating for any amount of time. This usually affects their work or school performance. Daydreaming is common.

Withdrawal. A person dealing with depression tends to withdraw from previously strong relationships. They will isolate themselves from others so that they can seclude themselves to dwell in their misery.

Suicidal behavior. Depression is one of the most common reasons that people consider suicide. Because depression taunts its victims with thoughts like, *It will never get any better,* depressed people often see removing themselves from the circumstance as a good option.

No matter what the reason is for the depression, and whether the intensity is strong or weak, depression is a dangerous entity in anyone's life.

LEARN GOD'S APPROACH

God does care. His eyes see every tear, and he hears every heart's sigh. Even when someone feels completely isolated and alone, God watches and he longs to send peace and hope to them. Although these strong feelings of unhappiness and despair will try to convince the victim that not even God is aware of their condition or concerned about their heartache, that is absolutely untrue.

Because God does care so much about us, he's even concerned about the emotions we experience. His Word is full of thoughts on the subject. Hopelessness, depression, and despair are looked at in many different ways. We get glimpses of people who struggled with these strong feelings and overcame them (King David being one of them), as well as God's thoughts on the subject as recorded by some New Testament writers. In the Bible, God goes out of his way to list the perspectives that led to depression as well as the tried and true ways to bring your emotions into balance. Let's see what he has to say.

"You are my hiding place; you will protect me from trouble and surround me with songs of deliverance" (Ps. 32:7). King David realized that when you are close to God, you are in a protected place. Not only is it physically safe, but it is emotionally safe as well. The songs of deliverance he mentions were not sung by God so that his enemies would be afraid. Rather, they were sung so that peace and hope would begin to rise up in the hearts of his people.

"I waited patiently for the LORD; he turned to me and heard my cry. He lifted me out of the slimy pit, out of the mud and mire; he set my feet on a rock and gave me a firm place to stand. He put a new song in my mouth, a hymn of praise to our God. Many will see and fear and put their trust in the LORD" (Ps. 40:1–3). Again, David declares that God was right there for him. He writes about the progress that he made from the "slimy pit" to the "firm place." David journeyed from depression to a place of security and health.

And he gave the credit to God. He says that God actually changed the condition of his heart so much that he began to sing a new song. And he proclaims that when people observed the miracle that took place in his life, they would recognize it as God's doing and put their trust in the Lord.

"Why are you downcast, O my soul? Why so disturbed within me? Put your hope in God, for I will yet praise him, my Savior and my God" (Ps. 42:5). Here the writer does an interesting thing. Going introspective and taking an inventory of his emotions, he realized that his soul was downcast and disturbed. After asking himself why that was, he didn't record an answer, but he did list a remedy. To move from depression, he had to put his hope in God. Instead of looking intently at his problems, he needed to begin to gaze into the face of the one who could help him overcome them.

"May the God of hope fill you with all joy and peace as you trust in him, so that you may overflow with hope by the power of the Holy Spirit" (Rom. 15:13). This is a beautiful prayer. To paraphrase, "May you be filled with hope until you are overflowing with joy, peace, and contentment." That is what God wants for your life.

"Rejoice in the Lord always. I will say it again: Rejoice! . . . Do not become anxious about anything, but in everything, by prayer and petition, with thanksgiving, present your requests to God. And the peace of God, which transcends all understanding, will guard your hearts and your minds in Christ Jesus" (Phil. 4:4, 6–7). God calls us to rejoice, and there is no reason not to. No matter how bad your circumstances look, there are good things on the horizon. Nothing bad lasts forever. If you are a child of God, you have hope and a future. And God has promised you peace. A unique kind of peace that goes above and beyond any circumstance and is stronger than any challenge you will face. It isn't dependent on your situation. Instead it is initiated and sustained by his perfect love.

"Cast all your anxiety on him because he cares for you" (1 Peter 5:7). You have permission to run to God with any care you have. When you're feeling overwhelmed, you can ask for God's help. If you're buried in depression, you can cast it up to him. If painful situations are gnawing at you night and day, God will take them from you. He wants to carry your burdens, but you must cast them to him.

IT'S TIME TO CLIMB

A life controlled by depression always lacks hope and peace. Despair dominates the lives of people who struggle to believe anything better will come. And peace is absent whenever anguish is present.

Therefore, the best way to chase off the strong negative emotions is to nurture these two positive perspectives. Here are some practical suggestions to make that more tangible:

Be thankful. People with no hope always focus on the things they don't have. They concentrate on the negative things going on in their lives and the catastrophes that rule their landscape.

To overcome this, you must stop looking at what you lack and recognize what you have been blessed with. A person who is authentically thankful will rarely struggle with depression.

Taking time to examine your life to discover the blessings you have is a good way to change your perspective. After you make a mental list of all that is good, thank God for granting you such favor in those areas.

Focus on worship. If your emotions are low, then you need to change what you are focusing on. Instead of looking at the crisis before you, look to God, who is both above you and with you. As you discover the power of praise and the intimacy of worship, you will find that it is impossible to dwell in your sorrow as you lift up your eyes. True worship chases off depression because it takes your eyes off of your circumstances and directs them to the one who is above all.

Fight to see the big picture. If you can convince yourself that God really does love you and that he truly is bigger than your problems, then you will have solid footing to fight through your depression. At first you may have to make faith statements such as, "God is good, and his mercy endures forever," but as your faith increases, your doubts will diminish.

In the big picture, God really is bigger than any problem you have. Your emotions will lie to you and try to make you focus on a small portion of what's happening. Your situation looks bleak because you are so close to it. That's why it's so important that you back up and realize that God is right with you and he is on your side.

Allow yourself to look down the road and realize that it will get better. Depression stems from the thought that things will never get better. If you are trapped into thinking that things will never improve, then your hope has been stolen. But you can cultivate faith by looking down the road and realizing that problems that are so overwhelming now won't be a part of your life in a few years.

Middle school problems disappear as you grow and mature. High school difficulties cease as situations and people change. If you are in college and you are wondering if things will ever get easier, you can be sure that they will.

Every season in life has its own struggles, but none of them remain forever. In the moment, you might feel like you're suffocating, but in reality you will live to breathe again.

Fight the urge to withdraw. Depression grows in isolation. When someone is overwhelmed with feelings of despair, they may want to withdraw. But if that is allowed, the seclusion will help incubate the negative feelings and allow them to grow.

When someone recognizes that they are starting to move toward depression, they can combat it by surrounding themselves with a healthy support system. By recruiting people who have godly perspectives, loving hearts, and strong discernment, depression will begin to give way. Because emotions tend to be contagious, this support system can go a long way toward victory.

The person who deals with despair must be aware of one danger here—the tendency to use emotion to manipulate the friendship and sympathy of those around them. When they figure out that they can get attention from patient, kind-hearted people, they might try to play that card again to see if they can gain the empathy of others. Fight the urge. This form of exploitation may work for a season, but it will eventually chase off the people you are trying to become close to.

VIEW FROM THE TOP

Depression is a serious disease that affects millions. Some hide it better than others, allowing themselves to give in to the effects of depression only when they're alone in their room at night. Others, however, can't live one hour without this virus poisoning their relationships, activities, and memories.

Those who experience depression wonder if they'll ever be able to experience happiness. They feel trapped in misery and ensnared by grief. But there is hope and there is help. Even if depression has been a part of everyday life for countless years, it can be overcome.

GAINING GROUND

Ask Yourself This — Do you deal with depression? How often? Have you ever talked with anyone about it? Using the list in the chapter, could you pinpoint something that causes your depression? How does your depression react? What principles are you going to implement to help you begin to overcome your depression?

Key Scripture — "May the God of hope fill you with all joy and peace as you trust in him, so that you may overflow with hope by the power of the Holy Spirit" (Rom. 15:13).

Ask God to Help — If you deal with depression regularly, you need to get your eyes off your circumstances and onto the God of all hope. Prayer is a good place to start. Begin by praying this prayer: *"God, I know that you're a good God, that my life is in your hands, and that your eyes are on me always. I recognize that you love me despite my failures and that you have a plan for my future. You will never leave me alone, and you will never allow me to drown in my circumstances. But I confess to you that sometimes my feelings lie to me. They tell me that it's hopeless and that I'm all alone. I need you to help me bring my feelings back into balance with what I know is true. Help me take all my* *thoughts captive and make them obedient to Christ. God, I know that you will deliver me. You will lift me up, and you will sustain me. Demolish my depression, and renew a fresh perspective, a right perspective, within me. I pray these things in Jesus' name. Amen."*

6

forcing yourself to forgive

Kelly was a great girl. She was cute, spunky, and playful. She had many friends, and she was fun to be around. However, Kelly had a problem. She couldn't forgive her parents.

The stories she'd tell of how her parents had treated her wrongly weren't the most severe tales I'd ever heard. As a matter of fact, they were pretty mild compared to the stories of some of the students in our church. Her parents had never abused her or verbally assaulted her. But as she told it, they had done her incredible injustice by favoring their oldest daughter and neglecting her.

Even though the complaints seemed mild, to Kelly they were not. She had been scarred, and as a sixteen-year-old, she was still struggling to win her parents' approval. She would have been happy if they had noticed progress she was making in school, but all they saw was that she wasn't the student her sister was. She was a black belt in Tae Kwon Do, but her sister was a third degree.

She tried everything to please her parents, but nothing did any good. They never paid any attention.

When I first met Kelly, I instantly liked her, but I knew something was wrong. When she walked into my church, she was moody and angry and had horrible self-esteem. And even though she'd begun a relationship with Christ, those things didn't change that much. For two years she worked hard to embrace the Lord and learn to walk with him, but she kept stumbling. She wasn't making progress, and it frustrated her tremendously.

It was then that she called and asked if she could come over to our house for a visit. The moment the door opened it was obvious she was upset. Although her mother had dropped her off and was waiting in the car to make sure she got in okay, Kelly ignored her altogether. Instead of turning around and waving as her mother told her when she would be back to get her, Kelly defiantly kept her back turned.

Now inside, Kelly began by telling Mary and me about the fight she'd just had with her mom. They had fought about spiritual things (Kelly's desire to be baptized), academic things (grades), and social things (Kelly's choice in friends). She felt that every area of her life had been pried into, and she was fuming.

After about twenty minutes of Kelly's ravings, I stopped her and encouraged her to look at the relationship as a whole. I asked, "When is the last time you and your mother had a conversation when you didn't fight?" Kelly couldn't remember. It became obvious to me that every time she saw her mom, she would recall previous misdeeds and rehearse former feelings.

We began to talk about forgiveness. At first she didn't like the conversation. She felt like she was being attacked for things that were her parents' fault. However, as we talked, she began to understand that she wasn't releasing her mother (or her father or her sister, for that matter) for the wrongs that had been done years ago. She'd been piling them up and holding them to her advantage for years.

As we talked I began to think that there was hope that Kelly might be able to get over the past so that the relationship with her parents could go forward.

As she left our home that night, Kelly prayed and asked God to help her forgive her family, and she made a promise to God that she would treat them better. Because she knew she had a tendency to speak abruptly to her parents, she said she would try to recognize when conversations were starting to heat up. In those moments, she would try not to get defensive, would control her emotions, and would speak softly.

Kelly responded even beyond my hopes. I had no idea how much she would profit from her willful decision to forgive her parents and try to see them in a new light.

Things began to change for Kelly. Week by week her family environment improved. As she took the first step, she started to see that her parents were trying to support her and communicate with her. It all started with her decision to forgive them, but it translated into a more peaceful life at home and more privileges as well. Along with forgiveness, she'd chosen obedience, and that was making a huge difference.

I caught glimpses of the progress whenever I talked with her about her home life. But I also watched closely as one act of forgiveness impacted her spiritual life. Up to that point, she'd always struggled in her convictions. Her faith wavered week to week. But the roller coaster became less severe after her decision to forgive. She started to grow in her relationship with Christ. Her devotional life became more stable, and the fruits of love, peace, and joy became more evident.

Amazingly enough, her entire life began to change as a result of her decision that day.

RECOGNIZE THE DROPS

I couldn't believe what I was hearing. Older people (a man in his seventies and a woman in her fifties) arguing about a conversation that had taken place three years before. One felt wronged, and the other felt misunderstood.

"Come on, I didn't mean it like that," said the man as he tried to defend himself. "You are taking that way out of context." The woman sat there silently until he spoke again. "Well, if you felt that way, why didn't you call and tell me?"

Finally the woman reacted, "Why didn't you call me?"

It turns out that this father and daughter hadn't spoken in over three years. They let a misunderstanding steal three precious years from a relationship that used to mean the world to them.

I am continually amazed when I hear stories and conversations like that. I can't believe people will allow little struggles to separate them from their friends, family members, churches, and support systems. The problem is that people feel they are right and everyone else is wrong. They feel mistreated, manipulated, and not protected. Everyone feels like the victim waiting for restitution, but they refuse to accept responsibility for their part in the demolition of relationships or forgive so that the mending can begin.

Houston, we have a problem! But it isn't just in Houston. It's happening in Seattle as well. And Denver. And don't forget about San Diego, Charleston, and Miami. And this condition isn't limited to big cities. Unforgiveness is destroying friendships in small communities as well.

Its effects are visible in families, churches, youth groups, schools, colleges, and any other place people gather. All age groups are guilty of it, and millions of people suffer because of it.

Unforgiveness steals from the person who refuses to offer peace, and it puts in bondage those from whom forgiveness is withheld. Physical bodies are affected with sickness, churches with impotence, and families with emotional leprosy, all because of forgiveness that is never offered or not accepted.

Is unforgiveness a problem? When there are mothers who won't talk to daughters and fathers who won't return their own sons' phone calls, I have to say there is. When minor squabbles drive a wedge between husbands and wives, separating them from any real communication, we have a problem.

But it's a problem we can begin to rectify as one by one people who love God and are willing to obey his commands begin to offer peace where there has been strife and forgiveness where there has been unforgiveness.

Learn God's Approach

Forgiveness is a major theme in Scripture. Not only does the Bible focus on the forgiveness that is offered to us through Christ's sacrifice, but it goes to great lengths to communicate God's expectation that we forgive the people around us. Forgiveness is a key component to many of God's promises. Let's take a look.

> "Forgive us our debts, as we also have forgiven our debtors" (Matt. 6:12). In his instruction on prayer, we can see that Jesus taught us to include a forgiveness component. We

are to ask for God's forgiveness as we evaluate our lives to make sure that we are offering it to those around us.

"For if you forgive men when they sin against you, your heavenly Father will also forgive you. But if you do not forgive men their sins, your Father will not forgive your sins" (Matt. 6:14–15). Our forgiveness depends on our willingness to forgive others. If we offer it, we receive it. If we are stingy with our forgiveness, it prevents God from forgiving us.

"Then Peter came to Jesus and asked, 'Lord, how many times shall I forgive my brother when he sins against me? Up to seven times?' Jesus answered, 'I tell you, not seven times, but seventy-seven times'" (Matt. 18:21–22). He was pious when he asked Jesus if seven times was adequate. However, according to Jesus' standards it was not. God's ability to forgive us never runs out, and we should always strive to forgive as many times as need be.

"And when you stand praying, if you hold anything against anyone, forgive him, so that your Father in heaven may forgive you your sins" (Mark 11:25). Before we go to God to find mercy or receive his help, we should go to our peers to get our relationships right. We're not allowed to harbor bitterness or refuse forgiveness.

"Do not judge, and you will not be judged. Do not condemn, and you will not be condemned. Forgive, and you will be forgiven" (Luke 6:37). Forgive, and we will be forgiven. Can you sense a theme?

"Jesus said, 'Father, forgive them, for they do not know what they are doing.' And they divided up his clothes by casting lots" (Luke 23:34). Can you imagine how difficult it must have been for Jesus to offer forgiveness to the people who not only mocked him, but crucified him? Yet he forced himself to not only offer his forgiveness, but ask God to forgive them as well.

"Bear with each other and forgive whatever grievances you may have against one another. Forgive as the Lord forgave you" (Col. 3:13). Just as God forgave us for all of the dumb things we did and for the broken promises we made to him, he wants us to forgive those around us. Amazingly enough, God doesn't hold anything against us. And using his persistent mercy as the model, God commands us to follow suit.

IT'S TIME TO CLIMB

Forgiveness is a command. However, it's never easy. Although we understand that it's God's standard, many times we struggle to walk in it. Here are a few practical tips that will help you apply what you know is necessary:

Be thankful for the forgiveness you have received. Let's face it. None of us deserves the forgiveness God has offered to us. We didn't just wound him in a moment of anger; our sins literally led to his crucifixion. Yet in the midst of all that we did to him, he still chose to forgive us.

When we remember all that God has released us from, it makes it easier to forget others' transgressions. But when someone takes God's forgiveness for granted, refusing to be thankful, then they tend to be stingy when it comes to releasing others for their offenses.

Recognize the other person's needs and wounds. On occasion you will run into someone who is just plain mean. However, most of the people who are rude, offensive, and irritating are dealing with issues. If someone offends you, there's a good chance that either they didn't intend to or they're walking through a rough season of their life. If you react emotionally to their actions without considering the reason why they did what they did, you may add to their already existing wounds.

God wants you as a Christian to help bring peace to others' lives instead of more chaos. Few are the people who are mature enough to stifle their personal emotions to respond appropriately to others, but that is how we are called to react.

When you focus on the other person's wounds and scars, it's impossible for you to feel victimized. You'll begin to feel for them as you selflessly take your eyes off yourself and think about someone else's needs.

Ask for God's help. Forgiveness is very difficult and totally against our nature. Because of that, it is imperative that we invoke the help and strength of God. By communicating with God openly and honestly about our lack of ability to forgive and even our lack of desire to do so (it's okay, we can be honest with him), we invite him to come alongside us as we strive to obey him in this area of our life.

Stop listening to your excuses. Every person I know feels justified in their unforgiveness. Because someone said something or did something to them, they feel that they can harbor horrible feelings and demolish relationships.

But if you're going to walk in God's plan for your life as you learn to forgive the people that wrong you, you must stop listening to your excuses. As good as your rationalizations sound, God doesn't accept them as valid reasons for your inability to forgive. You must overcome them.

Take the first step. Many relationships come to crossroads of misunderstanding. When this happens, someone needs to take the first step toward reconciliation. Rather than waiting for the other person to make that move, you should take it upon yourself. Pride will try to keep you in your comfortable little corner, holding on to your wound, but the Spirit of God will lead you to reach out and make it right.

Step out. Apologize for any wounds you have inflicted or mis-understandings you have caused. Offering an apology is the first step toward reconciliation.

Be quick to forgive and swift to ask forgiveness. Living forgiveness must become habitual. It's a lifestyle where you refuse to let minor things add up to major misunderstandings. By refusing to take offense and by being quick to forgive, you do your part in being a godly influence in your relationships.

VIEW FROM THE TOP

Healthy relationships make life more fulfilling, while damaged friendships make it frustrating. Even though you may feel justified in holding on to and rehearsing past wrongs, wisdom says you will be happier if you let them go and get over it.

Living a life of forgiveness takes work, patience, and God's help. It won't come naturally for you, but the benefits will prove to be more than worth the work. Don't let unforgiveness steal even one relationship from you. Every relationship is important and precious.

GAINING GROUND

Ask Yourself This — Do you hold grudges? Do you have problems forgiving people for ways they have wronged you? Are there certain people you struggle to forgive more than others? Who? Do you tend to take God's forgiveness for granted? Do you think it was difficult for Jesus to ask for forgiveness for the ones who were crucifying him on the cross? Are there any actions you need to take related to issues of forgiveness? What are you going to do and when?

Key Scripture—"Bear with each other and forgive whatever grievances you may have against one another. Forgive as the Lord forgave you" (Col. 3:13).

Ask God to Help—There are few things more difficult for us as humans than forgiving people who have wronged us or wounded us. Yet God asks us—no, he commands us—to do it. Therefore, we can be sure that he will help us if we ask him and trust him. You can start with this prayer: *"God, I need your help. I know that you want me to forgive the people in my life who have hurt me, but I struggle to do that. Actually, a large part of me doesn't want to at all. But because I want to please you, I want to obey. Could you help me to forgive even when I don't feel like it? And not just say the words, but really release it in my heart. God, thank you for forgiving me for all I have done wrong. Don't let me take that for granted. Always keep an accurate picture of the cross before me, because I know you bore the cross so that you could bury my guilt. I love you. Amen."*

addictions

7

ambushing
innocence

Megan is a godly young lady who has never dated, yet sexual images continue to cloud her mind. Although it seemed innocent at the time, when she went web surfing with two of her friends after school, destructive seeds were planted in her mind.

These three Christian girls responded that afternoon with innocent giggles, not lustful oohs and aahs. And they rationalized their behavior by saying that they just wanted to see what all the fuss was about. However, their innocence took a hit that day.

Megan would love to forget the things that she saw that day, but she can't.

Jeff never considered himself a lustful person, but he's always been curious. His environment growing up was much more protected than that of most of the friends he'd grown up with. They'd been exposed to sexual images and ideas through their music, movies, and conversations. In turn, those sexual ideas had become a part of their life philosophies. But not for Jeff.

He'd grown up in a Christian home with a strong desire to walk closely with God. Jeff had chosen to not date in high school; instead he'd embraced the concept of courtship. He'd actually gone a step further, deciding that he wouldn't even kiss a girl until his wedding day. So how had pornography trapped him?

While Jeff was riding in the car with some of his friends from youth group, the conversation turned sour. They began to discuss the girls in their group, making comments none of them intended to follow through with but which seemed to get a laugh. Nervously, Jeff spoke up. "You know, guys, we shouldn't be talking like this." The simple fact that someone was willing to speak up silenced them all. Their consciences returned, and they changed the subject. But the damage had been done.

Jeff had heard things that day that had made him think. He'd never gone exploring on the Internet before, but his curiosity about the female body and the rumors he'd heard about how easy it was to access pictures called out to him later that evening. Although he'd gone to bed early, his mind was racing and he couldn't drift off to sleep. Sometime around midnight he got out of bed, turned on his computer, and went exploring. He wasn't planning on looking long. He was just going to look at a few pictures, but before he knew where the time had gone, it was five in the morning.

Dejected and discouraged, he shut off the computer and crawled back into bed. He felt dirty. This was a new sensation and a disturbing one. For a long time he lay in bed with his mind racing and his convictions battling his shame. He'd known better, but he'd still given in. Finally he drifted off to sleep, but his life was forever altered.

Jeff is now in college, training for ministry, but he still hears the silent cries of his computer calling to him to log on and look around. Although he's usually able to run from those temptations, once in a while he gives in. And the images that are stuck in his mind come back to visit at the most inconvenient times.

Barry didn't go looking for pornographic material, but he didn't get up and leave when it came to find him. While spending the night at a friend's house when he was thirteen, he watched an X-rated movie that proved costly to his moral fiber.

His friend thought that Barry would be impressed if he pulled out what the "big boys" watch. And although he wasn't impressed, Barry didn't follow his conscience and speak up, nor did he walk out. He was shocked by what he saw but paralyzed by his embarrassment. He didn't want his friend to think he wasn't sexually progressive. So he sat there.

Barry now realizes that his mind has been impacted by those images for a couple of years. And although he was horrified at pornography when he first saw it, he is now addicted. When he watched that first tape, he was naïve, but not anymore. He has made several mistakes in relationships by surrendering his innocence early and sacrificing spiritual convictions for physical intimacy. Even though he now wants to embrace God's plan for his purity, the guilt he feels makes it difficult to believe that God could ever love him or restore what he has lost.

Some friends of mine were caught off guard when they realized their fourteen-year-old baby-sitter, who attended their church, had been using their computer to visit pornographic sites.

As they lovingly confronted this teenager and her mother, the daughter cringed, while the mother expressed shock. To her credit, the young lady didn't try to lie about it; however, her first reaction was to offer excuses. Turning to her mom with tears flowing, the baby-sitter said, "Ever since Dad has been gone, things have been hard."

For several minutes the mother and daughter talked. Graciously and tenderly, the mother handled her daughter's emotional outbursts. She hugged her and talked affectionately to her, but she didn't let her use excuses. Calling her by name, she said, "Now, you know better. You know those images aren't good for you." My friend and his wife stayed out of the conversation as the two on the couch worked toward forgiveness.

After all the tears had stopped and the conversation had stalled, my friend stepped in and said, "You know we love you, and that isn't going to change. We want you to know that you aren't allowed to avoid us because of the guilt and shame you might feel when you see us."

Amazingly, the two families are now several months past this episode and things are quite healthy. The girl still baby-sits for them. Now that her struggles have come to light, she is walking through them with her mother. And this couple continues to be a part of her life. For accountability's sake, they will occasionally ask if she's doing okay. And when she sees the sincerity on their faces, she knows they aren't asking a shallow question. They're checking on her to make sure that she has somewhere to turn if she begins to deal with those temptations again. Unembarrassed, she honestly declares that things are going well. She continues to fight, but with the help of God and her mother, she's winning the battle.

RECOGNIZE THE DROPS

Although I would love to tell you that the gravitational pull of pornography is weakening, it is not. With the emergence of the Internet making dangerous materials readily available to people of all ages, pornography has increased its influence. It has particularly affected the younger generations, even churchgoing young people.

- In a survey of students in middle school and above, 91 percent of males said that they had been exposed to pornographic materials.[1]
- In the same survey, 82 percent of females said that they had been introduced to the same material.[2]
- In a survey of Christian teens, 16 percent had viewed a movie with an X rating within the past three months.[3]

Whether drawn in by curiosity or caught off guard by images that pop up unexpectedly, thousands of people of all ages, backgrounds, and religious beliefs are becoming victims of the deadly disease of pornography.

Although he felt called to ministry and a commitment to protect his virginity, Steve was addicted to the pornographic images that were available in the quietness of his bedroom. Although his room should have been a place where he drew closer to God and guarded his purity, it was the very place where he was drawing away to destroy it.

When Steve and I went out for a meal, I had no intention of talking about these hidden areas of his life, but it was obvious that he was struggling. So I broached the subject. Although he wanted to deny it, the questions were so direct that he was aware that I'd read him. Finally he admitted his addiction. "I don't know why I do it. I don't even like it. I feel dirty, and those pictures don't ever fulfill me. As a matter of fact, most of the time they disgust me. I've tried to stop, but I can't. Something keeps drawing me back there."

After he had vented and confessed, he asked what could be done. Together we set up a system to hold him accountable to having his times alone with God, and then we made plans to meet together regularly. I told him that I wouldn't judge him but I would help him overcome this obstacle. I told him he must be willing to be dangerously honest with me. I told him that when I asked if he'd struggled with lust or pornography, he had to tell me the truth. I told him that kind of transparency is difficult, but it would be necessary if he wanted to conquer his problem. He agreed.

It's been several years since that first conversation. And although Steve will tell you how embarrassed he was as we were walking through that first encounter, he will also tell you that he is glad we had that talk. Because he accepted help and was willing to work to change his habits, he is headed in the right direction. He is protecting his purity, and he is holding on to God's standards for morality. He has no idea what his life would look like if he had continued to hide his problem, but he likes where he is now and the direction he is heading.

LEARN GOD'S APPROACH

Although the word *pornography* can't be found in the Bible, Scripture does have a lot to say about morality and holiness. God makes it clear that our responsibility is to protect our innocence, treat others with absolute purity, and think about only wholesome things. Here are just a few Scriptures that discuss these concepts, which we can relate to specific areas of our lives.

"I made a covenant with my eyes not to look lustfully at a girl" (Job 31:1). Even back in Job's day, some people had problems with their wandering eyes getting them in trouble. Recognizing that his lustful thoughts began with improper images, he resolved not to allow his eyes to look wrongly at females.

"Finally, brothers, whatever is true, whatever is noble, whatever is right, whatever is pure, whatever is lovely, whatever is admirable—if anything is excellent or praiseworthy—think about such things" (Phil. 4:8). Scripture gives us an outline of the right things to allow into our minds. The things that produce purity, those things that are right and proper, are the things that produce positive results.

"Do not rebuke an older man harshly, but exhort him as if he were your father. Treat younger men as brothers, older women as mothers, and younger women as sisters, with *absolute purity*" (1 Tim. 5:1–2, italics added). God's command and our responsibility is to treat everyone as family members we love, not people we exploit. We are to treat every relationship, every human being, with *absolute purity*. When we selfishly look at others in a way that degrades them, then we are not fulfilling God's command.

"Flee the evil desires of youth, and pursue righteousness, faith, love and peace, along with those who call on the Lord out of a pure heart" (2 Tim. 2:22). Rather than fixing our attention on the things that feed the evil in our bodies, we are to flee from them. Instead of pondering improper images, we are supposed to run away from them.

IT'S TIME TO CLIMB

If you are addicted to pornography, you need to work toward getting free. With pornography comes shame that tells you that you will never be able to overcome this habit—but with God's help you can break loose from its grip. It will take prayer, accountability, and discipline, but you can conquer this compulsion. What will it take? What do you have to do to beat it? Here are a few suggestions:

Pray. Pornography is a trap that has been set before you to destroy you spiritually as well as to affect you relationally and emotionally. And because this trap is spiritual in nature, you need to fight it on spiritual levels. You can't win this battle on your own, but through prayer you can recruit the help of the one who holds the power to help you overcome it. Through prayer you can both strengthen your spiritual convictions and weaken the pull of the temptation.

Jesus taught us to pray, "And lead us not into temptation, but deliver us from the evil one" (Matt. 6:13).

Make a firm commitment. If you're going to break free, then you need to make an aggressive and firm commitment in your heart that you don't want to play games with pornography from this point on. From what I have seen, people don't begin to get away from pornography's pull until they actually begin to hate what it does to them and those around them. If you determine that you are done with this particular sin, then you can fight with everything in you to conquer this habit. But if you approach this battle halfheartedly, not sure whether or not you want to get liberated from the images, then you will surely lose.

Find accountability. Sexual sin festers in darkness. It lies to you in ways that make you think that you are the only one out there fighting this battle. The guilt works to convince you that if anyone finds out what you are struggling with, you will be either mocked or rejected. However, sexual addictions are best fought with strong, godly accountability strengthening our own discipline and joining with our prayers.

No one likes to admit that they are struggling with something as embarrassing as pornography, but you must get over the initial fear of seeking help. If you find someone who loves you, they won't judge you when you share this deep, dark secret. They will fight with you so you don't have to battle alone.

The best way to turn a friendship into an accountability relationship is to find someone (of the same gender) you respect as a godly friend and let them into this part of your life. By saying, "I'm struggling with something, and although I'm embarrassed to tell you what it is, I need your help with it," you are setting them up so they won't be caught off guard by the turn your relationship is about to take. After you make the initial contact and spill your guts, you can come up with a series of questions they are supposed to ask you weekly to help them hold you responsible for your actions. Try questions like:

Did you get on the Internet this week?
Did you look at anything inappropriate?
Did you treat everyone with absolute purity?
Did you look at any magazines that feed your lusts?
Did you watch any TV shows or movies that feed your lusts?
Did you spend time with God this week on a regular basis?
Did you pray about your habits?

These questions, or others like them, are a good place to begin accountability; however, there is one other element that is completely necessary if this is going to work: You must be absolutely honest with your friend. Even if it is embarrassing to answer truthfully, you have to do it. Otherwise this will become an exercise in futility.

Recognize when you are weakest. If you consistently stumble in your walk toward purity, you need to recognize when you have the most trouble. Is it when you are tired? Do you struggle more late at night? Is it when you are feeling lonely? If you can discover when the attack on you is the strongest, you can fight it more effectively. Take a quick look back and mentally map the times that your choices have been poor.

Take drastic steps to avoid pornography. The key word here is *drastic.* To overcome this habit, some people have to attack it with the same ferocity and aggression as they are being attacked by it. If you struggle late at night when you are all alone in your bedroom, you may need to move your computer out into a busier room in your home. Chances are you won't be looking at dangerous sites if you're afraid that your parents might walk in. One young man I know asked his dad to disconnect their Internet service altogether. When you are in a battle for your purity, no move is too drastic.

Renew your mind. To overcome pornography's pull, you must battle the lust and curiosity in your heart. You must change your thought patterns. An idle mind will usually lose the battle with immorality, but one that is actively investing in putting pure, true, and good thoughts into your life will win. If you want to overcome this habit, you must work to renew your mind by ingesting the Word of God. It is like a vitamin for the soul. With each dose you gain strength in everything godly and inject a dose of poison into everything immoral.

I truly believe that the greatest tool against the lust that draws people to pornography is the powerful written Word of God that cleanses the heart, renews the mind, and halts the advance of the enemy's attacks.

Memorize Scripture. Memorizing Scripture works to renew your mind, but it also has another component. Mental knowledge is not the goal—spiritual victory over sin is. And hiding God's Word in your heart does give you victory over sin (see Ps. 119:11). When you memorize and meditate on Scripture, it is not only a defensive weapon against sin, it is also on the offensive. That chapter, verse, or thought spins around in your brain, cleaning the little corners that have been hiding improper thoughts.

VIEW FROM THE TOP

Over the years I've had strong friendships with many young men who have hated the hidden lusts that continually drew them to pornography and lustful thoughts. One in particular comes to mind.

As a young youth pastor, Jim knew that his habits were wrong. He had actually counseled the boys in his group to avoid the very things that he was embracing. Jim's addictions might not be defined as pornographic by most, but to him they had the same destructive effect. Some of the magazines that he was drawn to played on his desire to see female flesh. The ladies were not completely exposed, but they left little to the imagination. Jim was addicted, but his addiction made him sick. After a couple of years of sneaking peeks and living with the shame of a double life, he finally got to the point where he hated his sin, he despised his dishonesty, and he was grieved about the way that he was thinking about the young ladies both on the pages and in his life.

After trying one last time to fight it on his own and losing, he decided to call me and ask me for my help. After the uncomfortable confession, he realized that I was more than happy to both pray for him and help him. We talked about questions that would help me hold him accountable, and a few days later he e-mailed me twenty-one specific questions he wanted me to ask him at random times. He also laminated a copy and put it into his wallet.

For over three years I have been in an accountability relationship with this strong, anointed, charismatic leader. And he has come a long way. I can't take credit for his progress; when he started to cooperate with God to overcome his habit and increase his innocence, he started to gain ground in this area. It was not my wisdom or my questioning that helped him get free. It was his desire. When he finally got fed up with his sin and chose to fight with all of his might, he overcame.

You can too. If you have stumbled upon pornographic material and it has captured part of your heart, you can break free. It will take aggressive prayer, strong determination, and the help of God and others, but you can restore your innocence. And you can bring back your purity.

GAINING GROUND

Ask Yourself This—Have you been exposed to pornography in the past? Is it something you struggle with on a regular basis? Because pornography comes with shame that strips you of self-confidence, I have to ask you this next question: Do you really believe God can help you overcome this struggle in your life? Are you at the point where you hate this sin in your life and are willing to do anything to get free from it? If so, start thinking about what it will take. Do you recognize certain times in your life when you are most vulnerable to the trap of pornography? Are you already recognizing some measures you're going to have to take if you're going to get free from this vice? What are they? Make a list of three people who might become good accountability partners for you.

Key Scripture—"No temptation has seized you except what is common to man. And God is faithful; he will not let you be tempted beyond what you can bear. But when you are tempted, he will also provide a way out so that you can stand up under it" (1 Cor. 10:13).

Ask God to Help—Because pornography is an attack against your spiritual life as much as it is against your mind, you need to fight back in the spiritual realms. If you are struggling with pornography, then you need to pray this prayer: "*God, you know my life. You know that I struggle with pornography. I confess it to you right now as a sin, and I ask you to forgive me. But I need more than forgiveness; I need help. I am desperate. I can't overcome this on my own. But, God, I know that with you I can do anything. Help me, Lord. Give me the strength to fight against this sin, and even when I don't think I have the strength, rescue me. I pray this in the name of Jesus Christ. Amen.*"

8

it only takes one

Jason never had a drink of alcohol until his junior year in high school. Although it was available to him through friends and acquaintances, his personal convictions kept him from ever experimenting with it. However, as the new school year began, he started accepting invitations to parties where booze was a part of the festivities. For the first few weekends, he didn't drink anything. He was just there for the fun. Some part of him actually enjoyed watching people as they began to lose their inhibitions in their alcohol. When people asked if he wanted a beer, he was quick to turn down their offers.

But that all changed in mid-October when he rationalized having his first beer—*One beer isn't going to hurt me. And if they see me drink one, they'll probably stop pressing me to drink.* So, with the intent of drinking just one, he tasted his first beer. His initial thought was that the smell was nasty and the taste was overrated. He wanted to put it down and never taste it again, but he was afraid of what everyone else would think. So he quickly finished it.

When he set the empty can on the counter, the host of the party quickly put another into his hand. Again, he didn't want it, but he didn't want to say no either, so he popped the top and began to drink. Before that night was over, he had downed four beers.

As he drove home, he decided that beer wasn't so bad. But he decided that it had to stop there. He wasn't going to turn into one of those guys who craved hard liquor and routinely got drunk. He determined that he would never try any alcohol other than beer.

That conviction lasted exactly one week, because at the next party someone offered him something harder. At first he said no, but when several of his friends began to pass around the bottle, he chose to join them. *If they can handle it, then I can too*, he thought.

Another week passed and a new Jason began to emerge. His reputation was beginning to grow as he became the comedian daredevil who was willing to try anything when he was drunk. From that point on he was a regular at the keg, the one to initiate the drinking games, and the one who brought and consumed a good portion of the alcohol at his friends' parties.

His legend spread so quickly that the entire school began to treat him differently. He was an idol to many of the guys, and he instantly became more attractive to many of the girls. Realizing that the changes in his status had begun right around the time he'd begun to drink, he knew he could never stop. His insecurities reminded him, *They all like you better when you're drunk than when you're sober.*

For two years he allowed his addictions to grow. It got to the point where he would begin the day with alcohol because he didn't want to walk the halls of his school without its influence. Although he'd promised himself that he wouldn't try any drug, he encountered marijuana. That proved to be another addiction. Then it was harder drugs. He got to the point where he couldn't have a real conversation, take a test, go to work, or have fun without some outside influence.

Yet Jason didn't recognize that he had a problem. Whenever his parents or friends tried to talk to him about his dependence, he would get mad and run toward more destructive substances.

As his high school career came to a close, he chose his college based on the party scene. And if it hadn't been for a wake-up call that came in his first semester, he might have wasted his entire college experience on substances, shallow relationships, and parties. But, thankfully, that wake-up call did come.

One fall Friday night, Jason hopped in his car and headed for his hometown. His goal was to get home and party with all his old friends who idolized him and fed his ego. But he never made it home. As he was driving into town, he got pulled over for speeding. Noticing the open beer can next to him, the officer had Jason get out of the car. He didn't pass the sobriety test. But things got worse. As the officer rummaged through Jason's car, he discovered some drugs. Jason was taken into custody and prepped for a night in jail.

That night Jason couldn't sleep. He was forced to retrace his journey. He thought about his first beer, his first stiff drink, and his first joint. In light of all of those things, he then examined his relationships. Before long he was searching even further in his history for his convictions. He remembered his relationship with Christ, which used to be so precious to him, and the promises he had made as a result of his commitment to Christ. As Jason sat in the cold cell that night, he wondered where he had gone wrong. And he did something he hadn't done in a long time. He prayed. He asked for the Lord's help. God answered with his presence.

That night Jason's heart was turned back to God. He decided right there that things had to change. He had to get back to the place where he used to be. His wake-up call reminded him of his Savior and his friend.

Although it's been over two years since Jason spent the night in that cell, he hasn't stopped talking to God. With firm determination he has held to his promise to abstain from alcohol and drugs. And he's still walking out his promise to live close to God and give his life for God's purposes. Jason is now a junior in college. And even though he's still considered a daredevil comedian who will entertain the crowd, a couple of things are different about him. First of all, he doesn't need a beer in his hand to help him express his personality. And he's also more loving. On his college campus he's known as an authentic and caring individual who loves God and serves other people.

Jason has come a long way. He often tells the testimony of how he got into trouble and then got out of it, and it has been helpful to several people who were making the same mistakes or being tempted to. But as grateful as he is that God has delivered him from those struggles, Jason still wishes he'd never gotten started. If he could do it all over again, he would never take that first drink.

RECOGNIZE THE DROPS

Alcohol is definitely a problem for many students in America. And sometimes those students become adults with difficulties as well. Alcohol goes hand in hand with many ruined marriages, abused children, and lost jobs. Although you might think I'm being too melodramatic, I have personally seen the effects of drinking problems, and I don't want to see anyone else live through the horrible consequences that come with them.

Fred is spending time in prison because he got into a fight with his wife after coming home from the bar. He threatened her with a knife. Darrin is struggling to keep a job because he has problems getting up in the morning after he goes out each night for what he claims will be "just one drink." Sue and her husband are separated because she wants the right to drink alcohol more than she wants to protect her falling-apart marriage. Ian and I met in another country. He approached me with a bandaged hand after getting into a fight in the bar. He asked if I could give him money so that he could get back to the United States. All of his money had gone into his drinking.

Then there are the victims of other people's drinking habits. Morgan wonders where her dad is every evening. And even when she does see him, she wonders why he always wants to sleep instead of play with her. Martha prays faithfully for her husband, with whom she shares a bed and a last name but not a relationship. Alcohol has taken her place. Keith's father is in prison. Because he got in a bar fight and seriously injured a drunk man, Keith was forced to grow up without a dad. Beth endured a night of hell and the memories that come with it when some of her drinking buddies raped her.

The consequences of the alcohol abuse crisis are severe. So how do we avoid them? Drinking in excess is the problem, but many habits begin as soon as the first drink is accepted. And first drinks are coming early for many in the United States.

- 90 percent of high school seniors say that they have experimented with alcohol in the past, [1] and 67 percent have experimented in the last month. [2]
- 88 percent of eighth-graders say they have experimented with alcohol. [3]
- 84 percent of eighth-graders say it is fairly easy to get alcohol. [4]
- 36 percent of fourth-graders say they have been pressured to drink in the past. [5]
- There are 3.3 million teenage alcoholics in the United States. [6]

Is alcohol a problem? Absolutely. Young people who have direction, purpose, and destiny make horrible mistakes with drinking and end up trading their potential for the problems that come with alcohol. Some are injured or cause injury as they operate vehicles while under the influence. Others do severe damage to relationships. The real tragedy of others' stories won't be visible for a few more years. But after their habits have been formed and the sequence of destructive behaviors has begun, the consequences of poor choices and weak convictions begin to surface.

Although some justify their choices in regard to alcohol, when you look at the big picture of life, the dangers speak louder than the benefits.

LEARN GOD'S APPROACH

First of all, you need to understand that God has standards and rules for a reason. Every law he has ever given comes from his desire to see everyone know him personally, live a full life, and be protected. His standards are not random values that he uses to control humans; they are carefully thought-out boundaries to shield people from destructive behaviors and tendencies.

For this reason, we need to know what God says. To do that, we must turn to the Word of God.

> "Wine is a mocker and beer a brawler; whoever is led astray by them is not wise" (Prov. 20:1). Some people become addicted to alcohol and are "led astray" by it. God makes it clear that this is not the correct path for a Christian because it is not wise.

> "Do not join those who drink too much wine" (Prov. 23:20). Wisdom requires us to choose our friends wisely. Some groups

of people socialize mostly when the alcohol is flowing freely. God's Word indicates that these are not the groups you should strive to be a part of.

"Who has woe? Who has sorrow? Who has strife? Who has complaints? Who has needless bruises? Who has bloodshot eyes? Those who linger over wine, who go to sample bowls of mixed wine" (Prov. 23:29–30). Some of the most desperate people are those who drink to excess. Their alcohol causes them unnecessary difficulties. Don't get caught up in that lifestyle. Although many believe the illusion that drinking will allow you to escape from your problems, the truth is that it adds to them.

"Do not gaze at wine when it is red, when it sparkles in the cup, when it goes down smoothly! In the end it bites like a snake and poisons like a viper. Your eyes will see strange sights and your mind imagine confusing things" (Prov. 23:31–33). Alcohol comes back to bite you. This proverb paints a vivid picture of what drunkenness will do. It will affect what you see, your ability to concentrate, and your imagination. An obsession with alcohol will poison your life in many ways.

"Woe to those who rise early in the morning to run after their drinks, who stay up late at night till they are inflamed with wine" (Isa. 5:11). Sadness and despair will come upon those who have addictions to alcohol.

"Everyone must submit himself to the governing authorities, for there is no authority except that which God has established. The authorities that exist have been established by God. Consequently, he who rebels against the authority is rebelling against what God has instituted, and those who do so will bring judgment on themselves" (Rom. 13:1–2). Although these verses don't specifically address the issue of alcohol, the principle here must be considered in this conversation. Many teenagers get involved with drinking before they are of legal age. When that happens, not only are they damaging their bodies, they are rebelling against God, and they will face consequences. *All* authority is initiated by God, and he expects us to obey it. If you are under the legal drinking age, you must obey that law.

"Do not get drunk on wine, which leads to debauchery. Instead, be filled with the Spirit" (Eph. 5:18). More than likely this is the most frequently quoted Scripture used when conversations about alcohol come up in Christian settings. But please note what it says and take into consideration all the implications of it: We are not to get drunk or intoxicated with any substance, because God wants us to be *full of him.*

IT'S TIME TO CLIMB

Almost nothing is more tragic than a life of wasted potential or stolen promise due to an addiction to alcohol. If you or someone you know struggles with a fascination with and overindulgence in liquor, something needs to be done. You need help. Here are a few suggestions to assist you as you work toward change:

Know your convictions. I am continually amazed at the number of people whose philosophy of life is uncertain. Some never think through their beliefs and convictions and so can be easily manipulated by the devil and by circumstances. If you know how you are going to respond if alcohol is available *before* you are pressured to drink, you will handle the situation much better than if you just let it sneak up on you.

Resolve to hold fast. Some don't know what they will or will not do in a tempting situation, and others just don't have the willpower to hold to their convictions. Everything in life worth protecting takes determination, resolve, and perseverance. Without it you can have well-formed beliefs and strong values, but they will do you no good—because having staying power makes the difference.

Share your convictions with your friends. Most mistakes are made in social situations, with people around. So if you share your values with the people you are around the most, they can help hold you in check.

Avoid people who don't respect your wishes. As you share your convictions, you will run into some people who mock your decision to avoid alcohol. Some will go out of their way to either make you feel stupid for taking that stand or to get you to break your personal promises. Those aren't the kind of people you should spend a lot of time around. Changing friends is always difficult, but if protecting yourself from the dangers that are offered when they are around is important to you, you must make the tough decisions and stick to them.

Avoid places that put you in the middle of temptation. Again, it may seem difficult to avoid the party all your classmates are going to, but if you want to hold fast to your convictions and know they will be drinking, you won't go there. Your social life may suffer a bit, but you're much less likely to make a mistake with alcohol in a safe environment than at a party where the booze is flowing. And if your convictions tell you to avoid the party, chances are that some other people know they shouldn't go either, but they don't have the courage to stay home. By not going, you might be able to get some of your friends to join you in a safer environment.

If you are under the legal drinking age and are drinking—stop! According to Romans 13, disobeying authority is sin. So stop! Decide right now to avoid alcohol.

If you don't drink, don't start. The truth is, you will never have a drinking problem if you never take the first drink. Your social habit can't escalate into a full-blown problem if you never begin. So decide not to go there. The closer you stay to sobriety, the more protected you are. And nothing is closer than avoiding it altogether.

VIEW FROM THE TOP

To complete this chapter, I need to share with you my personal convictions about drinking. Although some Christians may believe differently, I want to be completely honest and vulnerable with you and tell you about my decisions and why I have made them.

First of all, I don't believe that drinking alcohol in and of itself is a sin. I don't believe that the Bible teaches us that an adult is being disobedient to God by having a beer or a glass of wine. Scripture teaches two main things about alcohol.

1. The Bible teaches that we are not to get drunk or intoxicated or use alcohol to excess (Eph. 5:18).
2. The Bible teaches that we are to obey authority (Rom. 13:1–2).

I believe that drinking is not a sin unless one of the two rules of those Scriptures is broken. But if someone gets drunk, they are going against God's standards and therefore committing a sin. And if someone breaks the law by drinking while underage, that is also a sin.

However, I believe that a third condition comes into play here, and that is in the area of personal convictions. As you walk with God, he will speak to your heart about the desires he has for you. The standards he sets for you will be different from the ones he sets for others. They are unique to you. You must obey them. If you don't, then you are sinning against God.

Let me tell you how this works for me. I believe based on Scripture that it wouldn't be wrong for me to have a beer, since I am over twenty-one and one beer wouldn't get me drunk. However, I believe that God wants me to live by a personal standard that doesn't include alcohol. Although I'm in my thirties, I have never tasted alcohol. I have never had beer, wine, or champagne. I believe that God wants me to hold back from drinking alcohol.

As with all of God's standards, his rule for me is not without reason. I am convinced that he doesn't want me to drink for two reasons. The first is that I have an addictive personality. Whatever I do, I do it to the extreme. When I eat dinner out at a restaurant, I can't have only one soft drink. I will drink as many as they will bring me. Sometimes I take this so far, I feel like I'm going to float home. I'm afraid that I would treat alcohol the same way. I wouldn't have one, but as many as I could. And this would lead me to drunkenness.

The second reason I live a sober life is my ministry. Because I work with young people who tend to rationalize things and struggle to filter things appropriately, I'm afraid that a student who looks up to me might see me in a restaurant drinking and take my example to the extreme. They might say, "Well, if Sean drinks, then I can too." And they could try to rationalize their own sin because of my drinking. So I've decided to not drink.

I am convinced that it is imperative that you obey the scriptural mandates to not get drunk and to obey the law. Although alcohol has an entrancing and curious effect on people, God's standards are always more fulfilling. If you obey them, you will live a full and protected life.

GAINING GROUND

Ask Yourself This—What are your convictions regarding alcohol? Are you willing to adopt God's strong views on the subject and live by them? Do the friends you keep and the places you hang out put you in temptation's way?

Key Scripture—"Wine is a mocker and beer a brawler; whoever is led astray by them is not wise" (Prov. 20:1).

Ask God to Help—Even if you don't have a drinking problem, you would be wise to ask God to protect you from falling into this trap that has tripped up so many people. *"Lord, you know my life and you know my convictions on drinking. You have seen what my role models have lived before me and you have watched my past experiences. God, I want my opinions to be based on yours, and I want my convictions to be strong. Would you grant me the ability to have healthy principles to guide this area of my life? Keep me from evil and even the appearance of evil. I don't want to get involved in alcohol simply because many people in my generation are. I want to live according to your plans for my life. Thank you, Jesus. It is in your name I pray. Amen."*

9

a real threat

Rob was a great athlete who had started three sports by the time he was a sophomore. But his favorite was basketball. His sophomore and junior years, he was dominant, arguably the best player on his team. As a wing player with good ball-handling skills, Rob was usually asked to take the last shot in close games. And in those situations, he was usually right on the money. He won many games for his team those years.

The summer before his senior year, Rob started hanging out with a different crowd, and they began to influence him. Marijuana was readily available in the group, and he began to experiment. Then, toward the end of the summer, he was trying cocaine and other drugs. He began to pull away from everyone who wasn't in his new group of friends.

Basketball season was different for Rob his senior year. Although he walked into the first practice assuming he would start at his normal position, he ended up losing his spot—not because someone got that much better and beat him out, but because he lost something in his game. No one won his position; he simply gave it away.

All through the season Rob struggled. When he sat on the bench as the game started, you could tell he wanted to play and was disappointed that he wasn't out there. But when he did get into the game, he was ineffective. He couldn't dribble well. His shot was off, and he couldn't defend. After a short stint on the court, the coach would call him back to the bench, where he would sulk. Part of his posture was pouting, but part of it was showing pure frustration.

When basketball season ended, he dropped out of school. No one knew what happened to him.

RECOGNIZE THE DROPS

Being raised in a very protected environment in a Christian home, I heard about drugs but thought that they were only a problem on TV and not in real life. I'd never had an open conversation about drugs with someone who had used them until I was in my twenties, and I had never been offered them until after I was married. Although I knew that drug addiction was real, I didn't believe that people right around me were ensnared in this vice.

However, things are different now. Over the years I have sat and prayed with people of all ages who have struggled with addiction to everything from nicotine to Ecstasy, from heroin to cocaine, from weight loss pills to prescription drugs. Because of the personal battles of some people very close to me, I now know that drug addiction is real. And I know that the problems it causes are serious.

Here are some statistics to prove just how serious the problem is in America.

- One out of ten high school seniors uses marijuana on a regular basis.[1]
- One in six high school seniors has tried cocaine or crack.[2]
- Nearly one out of twenty sixth- to tenth-graders has used cocaine in the last year.[3]
- 12 percent of students ages twelve to seventeen use marijuana regularly (at least twenty times a month).[4]
- Every day five hundred American adolescents begin using drugs.[5]
- The average age at which children try alcohol or marijuana is twelve.[6]
- Nearly one in ten students involved in an evangelical church or Christian youth group admits to having used illicit drugs in the past three months.[7]

Some teenagers who are experimenting with drugs would say that it's harmless, but it isn't. Drugs are both very addicting and very dangerous. Some of the effects develop slowly, while other effects are volatile, ambushing the unsuspecting victims. For the most part, drugs affect the body in a negative way, sometimes causing permanent damage to vital organs and systems.

Even if you choose to ignore or debate the physical effects, drugs can cause serious damage. The very nature of drugs (and the very reason that some choose to use them) is to take the user out of their normal state of mind, making them unable to control their actions and decisions and unable to protect themselves.

Consider Jason. I read about him in the paper. The story was printed when he was approaching thirty, but his problem began when he was in high school. Jason got involved with some students who used drugs. He quickly became addicted. Every weekend he was out with his friends, smoking something, popping something, shooting something, or snorting something.

In his early twenties, he realized that he was struggling, so he went to a treatment center and got help. After he was released, he remained clean for several years. But after a surgery he went back to his old addictions to deal with the pain. Although no one knew about it (he even fooled his wife), he was slowly losing control. He would throw unprovoked tantrums, and he would disappear from work at odd hours. His wife became afraid of him but didn't know how to get help.

One night after a fight with his wife, Jason went over the edge. Because the drugs he was pumping into his body were stealing his ability to think properly and make decisions, he did something incredibly stupid: He lit his house on fire as his wife was sleeping.

As the flames grew, he came to his senses. Horrified at his actions, he ran in, woke up his wife, and got her out of the house.

Then he went back in to try to put out the fire. However, the damage had been done.

The fire department showed up and finished putting out the fire, and the police were right behind them. They took him into custody.

As I read the article, I felt terrible for Jason. My heart went out to him. I haven't heard the outcome of his case, but as I write he is sitting in a county jail facing felony charges of arson and attempted murder, among other things. And it was all a result of the drug addictions he had cultivated since high school.

Every story of drug addiction is different. Some are severe and grab the public eye through media exposure. Others remain hidden from society but eat away at individual lives and families all across the globe.

Are drugs a problem? For many. Will they be a problem for you? I pray not.

Learn God's approach

The commands in Scripture regarding drug use and abuse are indirect, but they are clear. Words like *marijuana, cocaine, heroin,* and *pills* are not found in the Bible, but the themes of intoxication, honoring God with your body, and dying to sin are addressed. These principles should guide our lives, and they speak directly to the topic of this chapter.

> "Do not get drunk on wine, which leads to debauchery. Instead, be filled with the Spirit" (Eph. 5:18). The principle here for alcohol is valid for drugs as well. Don't let anything intoxicate you or steal your sobriety, and don't let anything give you an unnatural high, because it leads to wickedness.

"In the same way, count yourselves dead to sin but alive to God in Christ Jesus. Therefore do not let sin reign in your mortal body so that you obey its evil desires. Do not offer the parts of your body to sin, as instruments of wickedness, but rather offer yourselves to God, as those who have been brought from death to life; and offer the parts of your body to him as instruments of righteousness" (Rom. 6:11–13). When you offer your body to dangerous substances, you are offering your body to sin. Furthermore, anything foreign that controls your body, mind, or emotions takes control out of God's hands.

"Do you not know that your body is a temple of the Holy Spirit, who is in you, whom you have received from God? You are not your own; you were bought at a price. Therefore honor God with your body" (1 Cor. 6:19–20). If the Spirit of God dwells in you (as he does with everyone who believes in Jesus and surrenders their life to him), your body is his temple. You are to respect what he has given you because it is first of all where he dwells and second of all a gift to you. Principles of stewardship demand that you protect that gift from harmful substances.

"So I say, live by the Spirit, and you will not gratify the desires of the sinful nature" (Gal. 5:16). Rather than following our own impulses, we are to be led and directed by God's Spirit. Our sinful nature craves the "highs" that the world offers (not only drugs and alcohol but also power, fleshly satisfaction, money, and other temptations), but God's Spirit longs for us to be healthy, whole, and protected in a passionate relationship with him. We can only give our lives and bodies over to one of the two things fighting to influence us. We will either hand control over to our own evil desires or, by walking obediently, hand control over to God.

If you are trapped in a lifestyle that includes damaging your body through drug use, then you need to get free. Without intentional actions the battle will only get stronger and the perils to your own body and life will increase. However, with the proper attitude motivating your desire to change, you can overcome the strongest addiction.

I am convinced that there is nothing God can't do. And although people who are trapped in a routine of drug abuse feel helpless, God can break any bondage and help anyone overcome their addictions.

If you are trapped in addiction, here are some tips to help change the course of your life:

Recognize drug use as a sin and as harmful. Putting the poison of drugs into your body is dangerous. And it's a sin. If you are rationalizing this choice and debating the true effects of drugs, you probably really don't want to be free of their pull. When you realize that you are damaging your body and your relationships and grieving God, you have taken the first step toward beating your struggle.

Realize that this fight won't be won alone. Drug addictions are known as some of the most difficult addictions to overcome. Drug addiction is a battle that can't be fought alone. Although reading a chapter or even an entire book on the subject might help somewhat, freedom will come only when you have the help of someone with expertise in the field as well as people who offer spiritual support. To win, you must move toward three groups of people:

God. If you want to overcome a strong addiction or a growing habit with drugs, you are going to have to enlist the help of the one who has power over every addiction and is continually working to produce positive change in our lives. Through aggressive prayer, hand control over to God and invite his power and strength to invade your situation. Even the desperate prayer, "Lord, help! I'm losing this battle!" is answered.

Those around you. You need to find the people around you who really care about you and will stand with you to win these battles. When you find this support system and share honestly with these people, you'll find more strength to stand.

Professionals. I realize if you have a hidden life of drug addiction you may not want to get the proper help because of the embarrassment involved. However, people who try to fight these addictions on their own rarely succeed. Many organizations exist just to help people overcome their addictions to drugs and alcohol. People who find these professionals have a higher success rate in kicking their habits than those who refuse to get the proper help.

Replace your addiction to drugs with investment in your spiritual life. Instead of running to a temporary high that carries extreme risks and consequences, learn to build a strong relationship with Christ. Instead of depending on external things to pick you up, make you forget, or help you cope, learn to lean on the Lord. Although you'll have to apply a different perspective and some intentional effort, God can meet every need you ever have. And unlike drugs, spiritual growth isn't expensive, illegal, or dangerous.

Memorize Scripture. This may sound like a pat "Sunday school" answer, but memorizing Scripture is a powerful tool that you can use against any sin or addiction. The Bible teaches in Psalm 119:11 that when you hide God's Word in your heart, it helps you overcome areas of sin in your life. When you take time to read, meditate on, and memorize Scripture, you are taking action to ensure that you will draw closer to God as well as have the courage and inner strength to fight against the temptations that hit you the hardest.

Change your environment. Typically those who get involved in the drug scene do so because they are surrounded by people who are doing drugs as they hang out in places where drugs are available. If you know you have a weakness in the area of drugs, you must change some things. If you've proven to yourself that you're not strong enough to say no to the influence of your peers, then don't try to develop some hidden strength. Just start avoiding those friends. If you can't go to the clubs or parties where drugs are available without giving in to temptation, then avoid those places altogether. If you want to get free more than anything else, you won't argue with drastic measures. You'll do whatever it takes.

━━━ VIEW FROM THE TOP

Drugs have destroyed many promising lives. They have taken people packed with potential, held them back in their development, and left them always wondering what could have been. Drugs have killed many people and left other lives so empty that it was as if they were dead.

But there's hope. God has brought back many from the shores of death. Some who had been trapped, wondering if they could ever escape, have gotten free of the pull of drugs and moved so far away that they are no longer tempted by them. Even some of the things that had been taken from their lives as a result of their abuse have been returned to them.

If you or someone you know is dealing with drug addictions, it isn't too late. I am convinced that any person who is facing these issues can overcome them. Don't give up hope. Take the proper steps. Get the right help. Give God the chance to work miracles in your life, and you will have a bright tomorrow.

If you've never experimented with drugs, please decide right now that you'll never give them a chance to steal from you. Although the offers may come and the pressure may insist that you go along, develop your conviction against these substances until you are so strong that you will do whatever is right and resist their curse.

The younger generations are being introduced to drugs at a frightening pace — the statistics quoted earlier in this chapter prove that. However, you can be someone who offers hope for those who are trying to get out and strength for those who are standing against the influence of drugs. Be strong for yourselves and those around you. If you've never tried drugs, you can be a testimony, not of someone who God has delivered from severe addiction but of one who God protected from that first experience.

GaINING GROUND

Ask Yourself This — Have you ever experimented with drugs? Do you know someone who has? Do you recognize the physical dangers involved with drug experimentation and addiction? Do you recognize the spiritual difficulties that come as well? If you are going to get free from the pull of drugs, what changes do you have to make? Do you have someone you can talk to about this area of your life?

Key Scripture — "Do you not know that your body is a temple of the Holy Spirit, who is in you, whom you have received from God? You are not your own; you were bought at a price. Therefore honor God with your body" (1 Cor. 6:19–20).

Ask God to Help — As with the previous chapter, whether or not you are involved in a lifestyle that involves drugs, you need to determine now how you will respond in the future. God can help with that. You can pray. "*God, you are enough for me. Although other people need some substance to help them cope with their day, I refuse to do that. I want to allow you to control my attitudes and change my opinions. You and nothing else. For that reason I ask you to help me stand strong against the temptation to do drugs. Help me use wisdom when choosing friends. May I never pick people who will pressure me. Lord, I want to walk closely with you. Teach me how to grow in my spiritual life. In the mighty name of Jesus I pray. Amen."*

social
issues

10

Do i have to obey?

She came in with her guns blazing. She was angry with her parents, and she wasn't afraid to show it. Her voice rose every time she spoke, making it impossible to ignore her, but when it came time for her to listen to her parents' views, she refused. When she wasn't interrupting, she was rolling her eyes. On a couple of occasions I had to reach over and grab her hand and hold it to the table with mild force to remind her to sit there and let her parents speak.

Although her parents told me about the problems she'd been having at home and the disruptions she'd been causing to the family, they didn't need to. Within two minutes of seeing them interact, I recognized that there were some serious problems.

As the confrontations in my office continued to heat up, the family members were feeding on each other's emotions. I knew that something needed to change. Politely I asked the parents to wait outside as I took a couple of minutes to speak with their daughter. They agreed.

With just the two of us in the office, I asked what was going on. Quickly she told me how unreasonable her parents were. I told her that wasn't where I wanted the conversation to go.

"Do you realize that you're out of line?" I asked. "You have no right to treat your parents like that. You might think you do, and society might give you permission, but the Bible doesn't. If you say you love God, then you must obey him, even when it's difficult."

We talked some more about what the Bible says about parents and children, and then I gave her a strong challenge. Appealing to her mind, not her emotions, I told her that she had a choice to make. Either she was going to do everything she could to submit to God and obey her parents or she needed to admit that her opinions meant more to her than obeying God.

Although these conversations sometimes are effective and other times are not, this young woman heard what I was saying. She agreed to try.

We called her parents back in and shared our conversation and the conclusion we'd reached. After a short time of instruction aimed at the parents, we prayed together. This became the catalyst for some change in that family. Although it wasn't an immediate shift to a perfect and peaceful family life, it was an instant improvement as the student realized she had an obligation before God to obey and honor her parents.

RECOGNIZE THE DROPS

As a former youth pastor and as someone who has worked with young people for well over a decade, you can imagine that I have plenty of stories to tell about students who refused to obey their parents. But instead of telling you tales of others' shortcomings, I thought it would be best if I shared some of my own so that you know that I don't claim to have been the perfect teen. As a matter of fact, I was quite the opposite. However, I've become convinced that this obedience to parents thing is a major issue. And if Jesus truly is Lord of your life, you'll take an inventory to determine if you're doing well in this area.

Disobedience came easily for me. I had an incredible ability to get out of my chores when I was younger and to break curfews as I got older. One night in particular, I decided I needed to go hang out with some of my friends instead of getting home on time. Although we weren't doing anything wrong, immoral, or dangerous, I was still wrong. My parents had asked me to be home, and I chose not to be.

Not only did I disobey, but I regularly disrespected them as well. Because our opinions differed on certain things, I'd roll my eyes whenever they spoke, as if to silently tell them they were stupid. I'd walk away from them as they talked to me, and I'd argue instead of listening to them. I'd regularly talk about them with contempt in my voice. Although I loved them, I didn't show them the reverence God commanded of me or that they deserved. I was wrong.

Lying was another way I treated my parents incorrectly. Of course, we know lying is wrong, but when you aim your deceit at your parents, you're really doing damage. I'd lie about where I was, who I was with, what I had been doing, how I had spent my money, and many other things. I still am not sure if they were wise to my ways, but I was continually confronted with my habitual lying, and I wasn't willing to take the necessary actions to change it.

Not only was I disrespectful, disobedient, and deceitful with my parents, but I was ungrateful. I can't imagine how much that must have hurt them. Knowing that I needed a new pair of basketball shoes, my dad showed up at my school on a game day with a new pair of Converse high tops. The only problem was that they were canvas, not the slick leather shoes everyone was wearing that season. Although my dad had gone out of his way to do something nice for me, I failed to gather joy from it or express gratitude. In the locker room, I bawled out my dad for being cheap. He never said anything about my attitude, but I'm sure I must have wounded him.

If someone treated me as unkindly as I treated him, I'd lose all incentive to serve them, but my dad didn't. The very next day, he came home from work with a pair of the shoes I wanted. And I still wasn't grateful. I think I replied with a comment like, "It's about time you got it right."

Many times I struggled to treat my parents the way that I should have, the way God wanted me to. But on occasion I got it right. You see, obedience and submission are usually contrary to our selfish desires. That's when you must choose to do what's right instead of what's comfortable.

One summer night as I was hanging out with some friends, I called home to tell Mom where I was. What I thought to be a courtesy call turned into a chance for me to test my mettle. I had to choose whether I was going to do what I wanted or what she requested.

On the phone she told me that she had just checked my room and found that I hadn't cleaned it as she had asked. I was told to return home immediately. Deep inside I felt like my mom had just uttered those hated words you hear when you are playing Monopoly: "Do not pass go. Do not collect two hundred dollars." It was as if my mom was sending me to solitary confinement and I was going to miss out on all of the fun and fulfillment of a night out.

As I hung up the phone, I was confused. To be honest, I was really battling. Should I do what was right, or should I do what I wanted? Well, I didn't think long. I decided that I'd better obey. When I told my friends I was going home and breaking our plans, they didn't understand. But I couldn't explain it to them, because it was against my logic as well.

I got in my car and drove home. I spent the night cleaning my room.

Was it easy? Absolutely not. Was it the right thing to do? Without a doubt.

One of the trends I've noticed in the world today is a downward spiral toward disrespect. It affects every level of authority, but none so drastically, routinely, or harshly as parents. Some might say that the barriers that exist between generations are normal, but I'm convinced that we can't use that excuse if we're walking with God and longing to do what's right. We can't overlook the attitudes that flare up whenever our parents ask us a question or give us instructions. We must be willing to take action against it so that we can ensure healthy relationships and fruitful lives.

LEARN GOD'S APPROACH

I hate to tell you this, but God does have an opinion about how you treat your parents. His standards in this area are high, and his expectations seem demanding. But as Christians, we must realize that God would never ask us to do anything that we were unable to do or that he wasn't willing to help us do. Our first responsibility is to get a clear picture of how he would have us relate to our parents. And from there we must work to obey his commands. Here is what the Book says.

"Honor your father and your mother, so that you may live long in the land the LORD your God is giving you" (Exod. 20:12). We are not only to obey, but also to honor and respect our parents. If we do, we'll like the outcome.

"Though my father and mother forsake me, the LORD will receive me" (Ps. 27:10). Unfortunately, not everyone grows up in a perfect home. Those who are routinely disappointed by their parents should know that God is there to pick them up.

"A wise son brings joy to his father, but a foolish man despises his mother" (Prov. 15:20). Even in a very practical way, those who please their parents are wise. They have less stress in the home. They win more favor and more privileges. This proverb gives a very practical definition of wisdom in the home.

"Listen to your father, who gave you life, and do not despise your mother when she is old" (Prov. 23:22). God's command is to listen to and obey our parents. Because it is commanded in Scripture, it is not an option but a requirement.

"Everyone must submit himself to the governing authorities, for there is no authority except that which God has established. The authorities that exist have been established by God. Consequently, he who rebels against the authority is rebelling against what God has instituted, and those who do so will bring judgment on themselves" (Rom. 13:1–2). As we've already seen in previous chapters, we are to obey all authority because God put it into place. This applies to mothers and fathers as well.

"Children, obey your parents in the Lord, for this is right. 'Honor your father and mother'—which is the first commandment with a promise—'that it may go well with you and that you may enjoy long life on the earth'" (Eph. 6:1). This repeat of the commandment highlights the reward that comes from obeying parents—that everything may go well and that we might live a long life.

"Children, obey your parents in everything, for this pleases the Lord" (Col. 3:20). Do you want to please God? Start with one of the most basic ways. Obey your parents.

"But mark this: There will be terrible times in the last days. People will be lovers of themselves . . . disobedient to their parents . . . having a form of godliness but denying its power. Have nothing to do with them" (2 Tim. 3:1–5). In the last days, there will be people who look godly, but they don't have the power of God in their lives. Something will be missing from their spiritual lives, making them frustrated and unfulfilled. One of the characteristics of these people is that they're disobedient to their parents.

IT'S TIME TO CLIMB

Is disobedience toward parents a sin? Yes. The Bible makes it clear. But I think it's more severe than that. As we just explored, the Bible teaches that even disrespect toward parents is outside of God's plan.

Because we want to be like Christ and please him in every way, we must take action. We must figure out how to submit to

God by submitting to our parents. Here are a few suggestions that will help you move in that direction:

Submit to God. You'll find it much easier to submit to, honor, and obey your parents if you are first and foremost submitted to God. By an act of your will, you can tell God (and yourself, for that matter) that you're going to come in line with his standard for your treatment of your parents.

Do it before they ask. Let's face it. You know what your parents want from you. They make it pretty clear what they expect. So if you begin to answer their questions before they ask and do things before they request it, they'll begin to notice. If your room is their pet peeve, then clean it up. If it's your car, keep it clean. If they want you home more, make an effort to reserve a night just for family. Although you don't need to go out of your way to flaunt your compliance, they'll notice the change and they'll begin to reward you for showing such responsibility.

Ask for forgiveness. If you're like I was, you may need to go to your parents and ask them to forgive you for the times when you've treated them poorly. Tell them that God has been working in your heart and convicting you of your attitudes and actions toward them and that you're going to try to give them the respect they deserve. You never know; this might be the first step toward a much-improved relationship.

Take time to be with them. It really bothers most parents when they see their kids beginning to pull away. As you enter into adulthood (however you define that), there's a tendency to save all your time and energy for your friends and none for your family. If your folks have voiced this or alluded to it on any level, they're beginning to miss the relationship you used to have. You can curb that by setting aside time for them. You can reserve a night for you and your dad to go out to dinner and catch up. Or you and Mom can watch a movie together.

Trust me. If you initiate it, they'll be surprised. But they'll be delighted.

Learn how to communicate. Many relationships are damaged because people don't know how to communicate. Oh, everyone knows how to talk, but not everyone knows how to do it in a way that's understood. By mastering the art of communicating, you'll save yourself many headaches.

Make sure that you listen as well as talk.

Communicate maturely if you want to be treated like an adult.

Be completely honest and vulnerable.

Don't let your mind prepare your response before it's your turn to talk. If you do that, you're not really hearing the other person's views.

Don't let your conversations get emotional. Emotion-filled talks can turn ugly quickly.

Know exactly what you want to say before the conversation begins.

Don't let the conversation end until you know the other person heard you correctly.

If your discussion is about something important, take time to pray either before or after you talk, or both.

Remember that communication takes work. You shouldn't wait for the next crisis to try to figure out how to talk to your parents. In the end, you must be willing to obey your parents even if you disagree with their opinions.

Make it a goal to help others treat their parents well. It's too easy to jump on the bandwagon of someone who is verbally trashing their parents. But it isn't the right thing. You should never encourage another person to lie to their parents or to disobey them. Even if that means personal discomfort, you need to support your friends' parents.

VIEW FROM THE TOP

Being someone's child is difficult. But parenthood is hard too. I'm not sure which is more challenging, but I know that good kids make it easier to be good parents.

If you want to live by God's standards in every area of your life, then at times you're going to have to force yourself to honor and obey your parents. You're going to have to learn to communicate effectively with them and submit to their decisions.

The way you're allowed to treat your parents isn't up for debate. If you're being led by God, you'll do the right thing.

GAINING GROUND

Ask Yourself This—Do you have a problem with your parents? Do you recognize that this is a major issue in your life, one that God cares deeply about? Are you willing to swallow your pride and do your part to see things change? Can you recognize certain times when you struggle to obey and honor them? Do you need to sit down with them and apologize for your attitude and let them know that you're working to improve? Do you need to improve the communication between you and your parents? How are you going to go about doing that?

Key Scripture—"Children, obey your parents in the Lord, for this is right. 'Honor your father and mother'—which is the first commandment with a promise—'that it may go well with you and that you may enjoy long life on the earth'" (Eph. 6:1).

Ask God to Help—If you're like I was, you definitely need God's help in this area. Ask by praying: *"God, you have been looking into my family's life for years. You know the problems we have and the ways I've contributed to those difficulties. Because you know best, I need your help. I know that my parents will never be perfect, but I need to respect them anyway. Even when I don't want to, I know I have to because you require it of me. Would you help me? Put a guard on my tongue so I don't say anything wrong. Watch over my attitude so I don't let myself get bitter or spiteful. Lord, help me learn to effectively communicate with my parents. And let me say and do the things that will convince them that I really do love them. Thanks for loving me so perfectly. Amen."*

II

protecting
your purity

Steven was a Christian who was well thought of. He was a regular at church, and he went to all the youth group meetings and events. The younger kids looked up to him because of his testimony, and he used his influence to encourage them in their walks with God. His parents were proud of him, and his youth pastor praised him. But something changed. Around the time he began to drive, his passion for Christ dwindled but his Christian persona continued. Although his heart was growing colder each month, there were no visible chinks in his armor. As his spiritual life began to take a backseat, his social life jumped to a place of prominence.

His dating life began to take off as he became more relaxed in his commitment to date only godly people. The girls at his school had always been attracted to him, but now he was starting to enjoy their flirtations and advances. Stacey was the first one he went out with. During their three-month relationship, she began to lead Steven into physical areas where he had never before been. After they separated, another young lady with a past took her place. Jill picked up where Stacey had left off. Although both girls had offered Steven sex, he was able to stop himself before he gave up his virginity. But he was left with wounded convictions and haunting guilt. Several times in these two relationships, he told himself that he'd gone too far and that he would take a stronger stand next time, but the very next time they were alone, the pressure to "play around" was strong. During those moments he'd forget his boundaries. Each date turned into a make-out session with few boundaries.

The more physical his relationships became, the more he drew away from God and from church.

After he dated Stacey and Jill, he found himself attracted to Susan. She was a couple years younger than the other two and much more protected. He was the first guy she'd ever had a serious relationship with. Because of that, Steven changed roles. He became the teacher. It wasn't long before he'd taught her everything he had learned from his previous girlfriends, and there was nowhere else to go. Except to bed, that is. Even though it was against both of their personal codes, they ended up sleeping together.

The next day brought guilt and shame. Something had changed. An uncomfortable dynamic had crept into their relationship, and communication became difficult. Steven had both given away something very precious and stolen something that couldn't be replaced.

The good news is that the incident woke him up. He realized how far he'd fallen.

He has since returned to his spiritual roots and tried to reestablish himself as a man of God, but every day he remembers his mistake. Although they no longer date, every time he sees Susan, he's reminded of his failure.

But he doesn't feel the effects only when Susan is around. The experience affects every relationship he has. Each one is tarnished by those memories and influenced by his history. He has recommitted himself to being a spiritual leader who will date only godly young ladies. And he promises that he won't do anything more than kiss a girl until his wedding night, but by giving in to the temptation, his mind has been tarnished and the fight has become harder for him.

Karen grew up in church too. She was very outgoing in many areas, and she was a master of flirtation. She was convinced that she could attract any guy who was within two years of her age. And because she was particularly beautiful, she was usually right.

Although she gave off signals that implied that she was willing to do anything in a relationship, in reality, she was not. Because of her Christian foundations, she had committed to saving herself for marriage.

However, the guys she dated weren't convinced of this. Because her only criteria for going out with a guy were his looks, popularity, and money, she often ended up dating guys who weren't moral. She'd find herself fending off their aggressive advances in their cars or on their couches. And although she kept them in their place, vicious rumors about her behavior began to spread as the young men tried to impress their peers.

In Karen's sophomore year, she found herself with an undeserved (well, sort of) reputation of being easy, and she was attracting all the wrong guys. That's when Nate came along. Nate was *the* man on campus. He was a senior, and he was the dominant athlete at the school. As is usually the case, his accomplishments elevated him to an esteemed and revered status among the other students. Especially the underclassmen. Especially the girls.

That's why Karen was so impressed when Nate asked her out. Although they'd known each other for two years, he'd never responded to her flirtatious ways. But when he began to notice her (it was impossible not to with the way she dressed) and flirt back, she was smitten.

Their first date was in December. And because she was so used to this kind of treatment, she thought nothing of it when she had to defend herself as his hands tried to go exploring. That first night he backed off and apologized. He promised to respect her wishes and not to go any faster than she was ready for. However, that lasted only one night. The very next time they went out, the scenario was the same. He was aggressive; she was defensive. But this time he wasn't so respectful. He kept trying to get around her defenses. However, she won the battle and kept him at bay.

But their third date was different. Because his charms had weakened her convictions, and because being close seemed so right, Nate found the fight less intense this time around. She said no, but something in her voice convinced him that she didn't mean it. His persistence won out. Before the end of the date, he was feeling like the conquering hero, and even though she knew that she shouldn't be moving in this direction, she wasn't feeling overly guilty.

For a month this trend continued. As each date turned physical, her boundaries fell. She ignored conviction by refusing to think about her actions in light of God's will. But she was still standing firm in her goal of keeping her virginity. After all, that was the main goal.

However, Nate's charms and manipulation finally won out there as well. She slept with him.

Now she's alone. Nate didn't love her, although he said he did. He just wanted to use her. He didn't protect her; he only manipulated her.

Her aloneness isn't limited to not having a boyfriend. She feels isolated. She's also confused, frustrated, and spiritually dead. When she asked God to forgive her, he did. But she's having problems forgiving herself.

It's been only two months since she split with Nate. It's too early to tell which way she'll turn. Will she turn completely back to God and let him restore her purity and help her make wise choices in her social life? Or will she decide that it's easier being bad than being good and begin to live up to the reputation she already has?

Michelle didn't grow up in a Christian home. As a matter of fact, it was just the opposite. If she had to pick a label, she'd say her family members were practicing heathens. They didn't value purity as an option. From an early age, she was encouraged to date, and that led to promiscuity. She lost her virginity when she was thirteen years old and related to guys only in physical ways. Then when she was sixteen, she went to church with a friend and accepted Christ. As her relationship with God began, she came to realize that he had standards that he wanted her to live by, including standards for her sexual purity. So she began to reestablish her habits in God. She stopped dating for a season and just worked on building a relationship with her Creator. God forgave her for her past, and he began to restore her innocence. She established her boundaries and held to them. Her dating life became a testimony of her convictions and her faith. On her wedding day, she was able to look into the eyes of a wonderful Christian man and tell him that although her life had started out rough, she'd been faithfully waiting for him for over seven years.

Doug was a faithful church attender but a typical male. He ignored God's commands for purity. Instead, he played the field and found ways to have his physical urges satisfied. But as a freshman in college, conviction hit. One day as he looked in the mirror, he realized his hypocritical ways. His duplicity broke him as he realized he had ignored God. In his dorm room with a friend, he recommitted his life to Christ. That night he promised God that he would walk in complete obedience. He asked God to help him change the way he looked at and related to girls, and he made a covenant with God to avoid things that would steal his purity and pollute his mind. Well, he just graduated, and he's pleased with who he has become. Since that day, he hasn't dated the same way or for the same reasons. He turned into someone who encourages spiritual growth in the girls he dates instead of tearing away at their esteem.

David, on the other hand, kept himself pure. He grew up in a Christian home, but rather than just relying on his parents' faith, he had faith of his own. His relationship with Christ led to strong convictions about how he would build friendships with others. And although he was tempted, he never broke his promises or pushed his boundaries. According to some people, his social life was weak and uneventful, but he was willing to sacrifice the temporary joys as he waited for God to bring him something that would be more meaningful and long lasting. He's getting married this month, and he's anxiously awaiting the day. On that day, he will join his bride and they will become one flesh, and together they will discover the beauty of physical intimacy as they give themselves to each other in the confines of their new commitment.

RECOGNIZE THE DROPS

We live in a society that works hard to strip away our purity and destroy our innocence. The media makes fun of virtue and mocks virginity.

The younger generations have a huge uphill battle to fight if they're going to hold on to their morality. Their minds are being polluted with sexual messages, philosophies, and ideologies at an alarming rate.

Many factors influence us in these arenas. Here are a few dynamics that are attacking our purity:

Media message. Two things you can say about the media industry: It is consistent and it is persistent. Although I'm pretty sure television shows, movies, and magazines don't have a written mission statement declaring that the sexual corruption of our society is their ultimate goal, I'm amazed at how unified they are in their messages.

Between every commercial break, sitcoms, soaps, reality shows, and music videos bombard us with visual images of things that awaken our thoughts to how sexual our world is. On top of that, the majority of commercials use sex to sell, even when sex isn't relevant to the product.

Because the media influence is so extreme, many people are desensitized to the things that should shock them, and they're ultimately led into the things they should avoid.

Apathetic approaches to religious convictions. An aggressive approach to pursuing and loving God will ensure that a person stays close to Christ and far from sin. However, when apathy creeps into the religious position of an individual, they become vulnerable to making dangerous decisions in the area of their purity.

Loneliness. People who have experienced loneliness in the past are willing to do anything to avoid returning there. Therefore, their emotions easily manipulate them. Because these people long to be loved and they don't know how to receive what they need from God, they settle for an immature and shallow version of love from a person who is close enough to meet their needs.

Curiosity. Media messages and overheard conversations just build on the natural curiosity we all have about things we have yet to encounter. This strong curiosity leads many to places of compromise as they make unwise decisions just to get answers to the questions that are racing through their brains.

Incorrect and early dating patterns. Let's face it. In our culture people date wrong and they date too early. Instead of dating being a ritual people use to build stronger friendships and begin deciding what qualities they're looking for in a future spouse, they date for popularity, prestige, and significance. Add to that the tendency to get emotionally attached too quickly, and you have a recipe for broken convictions and sexual experimentation.

And we must consider the fact that people are overly anxious to get involved at an early age. In America we're finding guys who are sexually aware by the time they're eleven and girls who know how to relate to guys only on a physical level by the time they're ten.

Reports show that early dating leads to disaster. Girls who begin dating at twelve years of age have a 91 percent chance of becoming sexually active by the time they graduate from high school. Compare that with only 20 percent of girls who are likely to be sexually active if they don't start dating until they're sixteen, and you can see why the trend of growing up too early is contributing to sexual promiscuity.[1]

Peer pressure. Yes, there is a pressure to play the games and get involved sexually. In many circles, high school guys who are still virgins are laughed at and whispered about and girls who have held on to godly standards are not as popular as their sexually active peers.

The temptations are strong and the pressure is high, but God's standards still remain. His ways are always right. Even though it seems like not many people are still holding on to their purity, it is imperative that you do. If you give it away, there are many consequences. There are physical effects (you've heard about all the diseases and the possibilities of pregnancy), but there are also extreme emotional consequences to poor choices. Many people walk around with intense guilt and shame because they didn't hold on. (If you've made some mistakes in the past, don't be discouraged. And don't stop reading. Before we end this chapter, we'll discuss how to get back on your feet so you can run to God for forgiveness, compassion, and renewed purity.) Others carry around the broken heart that comes with the realization that they have given away something precious, and they don't even have the relationship left to show for it.

You must choose to live your relationships with God leading the way. If you follow him, you'll be protected and safe. But if you don't, you'll experience things no person should ever have to endure.

LEARN GOD'S APPROACH

The world definitely has a different philosophy on sexual issues than God does. Rather than look toward biblical standards and boundaries, our society has developed its opinions about morality based on convenience and what feels good.

As a Christian, you must choose to submit your rights and your actions to God and his will. The first step is understanding exactly what God thinks about premarital sex. Don't simply take my word for it. See for yourself. Let's see what God thinks.

"I made a covenant with my eyes not to look lustfully at a girl" (Job 31:1). Sexual activity always begins with lust. Before your body will act on it, your mind will dwell on it. For this reason, it would be wise to follow Job's lead and commit to not allowing your eyes to gaze inappropriately at anyone.

"Create in me a pure heart, O God, and renew a steadfast spirit within me" (Ps. 51:10). This verse could be expanded, personalized, and turned into an effective prayer. Something like this: *"God protect my purity and rekindle my appreciation for and commitment to innocence. Give me a strong spirit to withstand the attacks that will come."*

"Do not conform any longer to the pattern of this world, but be transformed by the renewing of your mind. Then you will be able to test and approve what God's will is—his good, pleasing and perfect will" (Rom. 12:2). If you want to know what God's will is, you're going to have to renew your mind. You're going to have to work to feed it good and godly things. If you do, the philosophy of the world won't infiltrate you and drag you to the depths of its depravity.

"Finally, brothers, whatever is true, whatever is noble, whatever is right, whatever is pure, whatever is lovely, whatever is admirable—if anything is excellent or praiseworthy—

think about such things" (Phil. 4:8). Again, your mind goes there before your body does. For that reason, if you can control your mind, you won't struggle with acting out in lust. This verse gives a recipe for things you can dwell on that will assist you in protecting your purity. Whatever is true, noble, right, pure, lovely, admirable—those are the things you should ponder, dwell on, and meditate about.

"It is God's will that you should be sanctified: that you should avoid sexual immorality; that each of you should learn to control his own body in a way that is holy and honorable, not in passionate lust like the heathen, who do not know God" (1 Thess. 4:3–5). It's God's will that you live purely and that you avoid sexual things. But you must discipline your body. This takes work but it's what God asks of you, and he will help you if you ask him.

"Flee the evil desires of youth, and pursue righteousness, faith, love and peace, along with those who call on the Lord out of a pure heart" (2 Tim. 2:22). If you have to run from something, you should also be running to something else. If all you do is try to avoid evil desires, you'd better pick a direction or you'll run aimlessly in circles. How about this? Run after righteousness, faith, love, and peace. If you're actively building those into your life, you won't stumble as your purity is assaulted.

"Be self-controlled and alert. Your enemy the devil prowls around like a roaring lion looking for someone to devour" (1 Peter 5:8). The devil would love to consume you. He would love to trap you and bind you up. But if you recognize that you'll have to carefully, prayerfully, and diligently navigate through sexual issues, then you'll have an upper hand. Mix that recognition with self-control, and your enemy won't be able to win when he comes near you.

Here's the dilemma. Some people reading this chapter have been able to successfully fight against impurity, while some have not. The statistics (even for Christian youth) lead me to believe that some people reading these pages are naïve about sexual things, while others are currently involved in impure relationships or have been involved in them in the past. Some may be wondering how to avoid these issues, while others want to know how to get out. Some might judge those who aren't pure. Others might feel judged by those around them, or they may be judging themselves harshly because they recognize that they've messed up.

Because of the diversity of needs here, I'm going to break up this section so I can address the issue from both viewpoints.

for those who have made mistakes

If you're one of those people who has gone where you know God did not want you to go, there is hope for you. There is forgiveness and restoration in Jesus Christ. He offers it freely; however, you must move toward him and away from the sins of your past if you're going to truly walk free from the traps that have ensnared you. Here are a few thoughts for you to ponder as you evaluate your life and get ready to accept God's help:

Ask God to forgive you. The Bible makes it clear that if you confess your sins, God will forgive you (see 1 John 1:9). I don't care how guilty you feel or how unworthy of forgiveness you are, God will forgive you. He promised to, and he never breaks his word. But you must seek his forgiveness.

Forgive yourself. Sexual sin can steal your dignity. It can leave you feeling worthless and dirty even years after the incident. And if you broke a personal promise, this kind of sin can even make you begin to loathe yourself.

Yes, God's forgiveness is easy, but sometimes we struggle to pardon ourselves for past transgressions. But you'll never be healthy if you can't forgive yourself.

Make drastic changes in dangerous relationships. If you're still involved in the relationship where you struggled to hold on to your purity, then you must make drastic changes. You must break up. Many couples have tried to embrace a newfound discipline and integrity in an old relationship, but habits die hard. Old tendencies will resurface. If you want to return to God's standards, you must make some major changes.

If you aren't currently in a relationship, then don't date for a while. Give God some time to work in your heart, renew your mind, convince you of how and whom to date, and let his love do its thing in your life.

I've talked with many students who knew conviction was hitting them hard, but they weren't willing to give up their boyfriend or girlfriend. They tried to stand against the pressure in the midst of the current that had routinely dragged them under. Regrettably, I don't know of one who actually succeeded.

If something inside you is fighting the thought of sacrificing a relationship so that you can resurrect your purity, maybe your purity isn't as important to you as you think it is. If holding on to your innocence is your ultimate relationship goal, you won't squirm when someone suggests that you take drastic action.

Apply all the principles below. Even though you've had some experiences that have chipped away at your purity, you must realize that restoring it and protecting it in the first place take similar actions. Therefore, as we move into the section for those who are striving to guard their innocence, you can be sure that these things apply to you as well. If you've asked God to forgive you and if you've reestablished your goal to walk in innocence, you have a clean slate. Yes, you have some memories that the person next to you might not have, but in God's eyes you are both right with him and moving in the proper direction.

tips to protect your purity

Set your standards early. People get into trouble in this area because they don't have strong convictions. They know they want to avoid the really bad stuff, but they aren't concrete in their thinking about the stuff between perfect purity and shocking sins. However, when you realize that God's design for you is that you aggressively embrace purity and that all steps away from it get you moving toward dangerous territory, then you will be willing to establish some firm markers about where you won't allow yourself to go.

Date only people who share your convictions. I realize that if you adopt this principle, you may be limiting your dating pool, but if you don't you'll surely get into trouble. Either you'll give in to your partner's wishes or you'll be constantly straining to fend off their advances. If you date only people who share your opinions about what is inappropriate, you can work together to maintain your standards of purity. These are topics you should discuss early on in a relationship.

Make definite plans when you are together. If you know where you're going and what you're doing, you'll avoid those awkward moments of inactivity where boredom drives you into tempting positions. If you're going on a date, make sure you know where and when. If you just want to hang out together and enjoy each other's company, make sure you go somewhere safe where there will be other people around. Checking out the bookstore, getting together at a coffee shop, or hanging out at a park are a few suggestions for sticking to safe places where you won't get into trouble. Or if you're looking for a cozy environment to just talk and relax, stay at home and sit in a common room so your family is around. Don't feel that you need to isolate yourselves from the world to be together.

Avoid certain places. If you really want to protect yourself, you'll realize that you must avoid certain places. Anyplace where you're all alone and there is no danger of anyone walking in on you should go on your avoid list. If no one is home, you shouldn't be alone with someone you're attracted to. Do not close the door to your bedroom when the two of you are in there. And under no circumstances should you allow yourself to be talked into turning off the lights. By avoiding the dynamics that increase dangerous urges, you'll be better suited to make wise decisions.

Bring back the blush. One of the reasons our society has begun to adopt the philosophy of sexual gratification as the ultimate goal in any relationship is that we have been desensitized. By saturating our entertainment with sexual content and by building humor around immoral things, we've been slowly moving toward dangerous territory for years. So if you're going to take a stand for purity, you must fight against these lying ideas and philosophies. You can't accept them as normal and allow them to overwhelm your thinking.

The most important element in protecting your purity is your mind (Ps. 4:23). When you refuse to take in sexual content, innuendo, and messages, you guard the doorway to your brain.

When I talk about "blushing," I'm suggesting that you refuse to look past the things in your life that would get you thinking wrongly. Make sure you evaluate the movies and television shows you're going to go see before you allow yourself to sit there and listen to their messages. Pick your music carefully, and use your influence to make sure that conversations with your friends stay safe and pure. It's time we allow ourselves to get embarrassed (and even offended) when something attacks our innocence.

VIEW FROM THE TOP

After the service, I went and I found them—two young ladies in my group who I knew hadn't grown up with the convictions that would keep them from dangerous relationships. I knew that after the speaker had so aggressively endorsed abstinence, they would feel judged or, even worse, like they weren't loved by God.

I was right. They were sitting in the hallway of the hotel. Both sets of eyes were misty, and they were quiet. They were sitting there in their shame and guilt, wondering if they'd been tattooed for life with the mistakes of the past.

I had to do something the speaker had failed to do. I had to tell them that we serve a wonderful God who longs to forgive them, even for their sexual sin. When he encounters even the dirtiest heart, he completely changes it and restores what has been stolen. I shared with them about God's grace and his mercy that would help them build a life free from the reputation and addictions of the past.

They listened intently, but in a moment of honest vulnerability, they told me they wished that were true but they had trouble accepting it. So many Christians had condemned them in the past that they figured God must feel that way too.

After many minutes of talking, crying, and sharing, our hallway moment was interrupted by the call to load the bus. Unfortunately, we never got to finish that talk. They never returned to our church. And it still grieves me to think that someone is running around out there not knowing that God can truly forgive them for their sexual sins because we Christians have done such a good job of communicating God's rules that we have neglected to share about his grace.

Although God does have standards for the way you approach relationships and the way you hold on to your purity, there's no way I could write this chapter without including forgiveness. If you've stumbled in the past, you must know that God longs to forgive you and help you get a new start.

Even though the world would love to convince you that your sexual sins are more intense and more difficult for God to forgive than other sins, that isn't true. The Bible clearly states that if you confess your sins, God will forgive them (see 1 John 1:9). That doesn't mean just certain sins. It means all sins.

Therefore, if you truly repent, you are forgiven and your sins won't be held against you. And for that reason, you must not let shame and guilt steal from you any longer.

GAINING GROUND

Ask Yourself This — Have you done a good job of protecting your purity in the past? Has your thought life been bombarded with images that make it difficult for you to think pure thoughts? Are there any changes that you need to make to hold on to the innocence you have left? Do the conversations you and your friends have make it easier to think and act purely, or more difficult? Are there any changes you need to make?

Key Scripture — "It is God's will that you should be sanctified: that you should avoid sexual immorality; that each of you should learn to control his own body in a way that is holy and honorable, not in passionate lust like the heathen, who do not know God" (1 Thess. 4:3–5).

Ask God to Help — In the battle for your innocence, you have no greater ally than your heavenly Father. He longs to come to your aid, but many people never invite him into this part of their lives. You can be one who does by praying this prayer: "God, *your intention for me is purity. You want me to stay as close to holiness as I can. There is nothing in my past that you cannot or will not forgive, so first of all, I ask for your forgiveness. Wipe away the guilt and give me the* *confidence that it is all forgotten. I need your help to restore the innocence that has been stolen from me. From this point on I will protect it as a precious prize that you have given me. Lord, thank you for being the God of second chances. I need you. In the name of my Savior, Jesus, I pray. Amen."*

--- 12

Does God Have
an Opinion
on Homosexuality?

I was horrified as the guest speaker was not only endorsing homosexuality as a valid lifestyle choice and discounting several scriptural principles, but making some outrageous statements as well.

The class was for a select group of students who were being trained to be peer counselors in the coming school year. I was there not as a regular participant, but as an outsider who had been invited to attend by one of the students in my youth ministry. My mere presence made the teacher nervous, as she was concerned that I might attack the guest she had invited to come and discuss the growing number of homosexuals in the school system. But I promised to only observe and not to speak.

For over an hour I sat there listening to the speaker and watching the fifteen students who were there. When the speaker shared that over 25 percent of the school's population were homosexuals, the students had as much difficulty believing it as I did. Then she shared her belief that every student in the school had, at some point, been attracted to people of the same gender. The class members disagreed, and their body language shifted so noticeably that it was obvious that they were shocked and actually scared by that idea.

Throughout the class, the speaker shared from her personal opinions, experiences, conversations, and preferences. When a student questioned her about the morality issues, she responded as if there were no right and wrong. When another student brought up the Bible, she wrongly stated that the Bible doesn't have any arguments. Because she sounded so confident, the students (even the Christians in the room) didn't speak up, even though her statements were false.

I was reminded of how aggressive and full of deceit the homosexual agenda is.

It was a date night for me and my wife. We decided to try a restaurant where we'd never eaten before. When we arrived, we were escorted back to a corner booth. Before we arrived at our table, we were greeted by our server. He shook our hands and introduced himself. Immediately something about him made me wonder. Well, my question was answered quickly as this man (let's call him Bruce) looked me up and down, then turned to my wife and said, "Don't worry, girlfriend. I'm not going to steal your man."

As you can imagine, I was shocked. I didn't know how to respond, so we fought through the next couple of uncomfortable seconds until Bruce went to get our drinks and Mary and I had a chance to talk.

Before Bruce returned, Mary and I decided that we were going to shower him with kindness. Instead of being scared or standoffish, we were going to ask him questions and try to offer him our friendship.

Well, it worked. Every time Bruce came back to our table, we would smile, ask him questions, and listen intently whenever he talked. Evidently, this isn't the kind of treatment that he was used to, because before he would give us our check he had a question for me. He asked, "What do you do for a living?"

Because talking about my profession opens a door for me to talk about Christ, I was more than willing to share with him. I said, "Well, actually, I'm a preacher."

With that, his eyes opened wide. He said, "I knew it. I knew there was something different about you. I knew you had to be a Christian." He then went on to tell us about his father, who is a minister. He even asked us to pray for him. "I know my lifestyle isn't pleasing to God. Would you pray for me?"

We made a friend that night. Bruce is still one of the people on my prayer list. I want him to return to Christ. And although I don't agree with his lifestyle, I'm convinced that God loves him and wants a relationship with him. And just because we're different in a major area doesn't mean I'm going to let that variation keep me from reaching out to him with God's love and forgiveness.

RECOGNIZE THE DROPS

Several decades ago an aggressive agenda came on the scene that has affected our culture in many ways. The priority was to introduce sexual freedom, experimentation, and promiscuity into our society so it would become the mainstream philosophy. Thanks to the media, which has bombarded us continually with the images and innuendos of sexual relationships, the agenda has succeeded. Our society has adopted a "sex sells" attitude, and many are living a "sex is everything" lifestyle.

The next area of infiltration seems to be in the area of homosexuality. There seems to be an assertive strategy at work to force our society to adopt this lifestyle as a valid alternative. Because gays and lesbians are gaining positive coverage in the media, this lifestyle is becoming ever more visible to mainstream America. Add to that the gay pride offensives, the growing climate of acceptance, and the encouragement and support the gay lifestyle receives in schools and colleges, and you can begin to recognize a well-thought-out strategy to affect our thinking on the topic.

Although people are allowed to have differing opinions on many things, this is not one of them. If you openly question the morality of same-sex relationships, you'll be tagged as intolerant, prejudiced, or phobic. Actually, half of the people in the United States say that those who are opposed to gay rights and the gay lifestyle are closed minded.

However, you would have to twist Scripture pretty dramatically to convince yourself that God endorses this alternative lifestyle, or even that he's unopinionated about the matter. Either those who say that people are born gay don't believe the Bible to be the inspired Word of God or they think that he is cruel and manipulative and creates people a certain way only to condemn them in the same breath.

The truth of the matter is that God creates perfectly but the devil perverts God's intentions and design. With intentional actions, the devil works to bind up the people God loves. One of his tactics is to introduce people to homosexuality. The shame and guilt that accompany this lifestyle make those who live it easy prey for the enemy of God to control and destroy.

For that reason, we must shed light on the deception that homosexuality is an acceptable choice that doesn't carry with it any consequences. We must not allow any more people to be deceived, and we must work to help free those who are caught up in this lifestyle. Although Christians have accepted the attitude that they should be scared of homosexuals, we must not allow ourselves to avoid them. By engaging them in friendship, by praying for them, and by sharing the truth of God's love with them, we can help set them free.

Learn God's Approach

Many people in our culture will look at the statements made in this book and determine that they are made by a closed-minded individual. They will assume that I'm a "hater." I strongly disagree. Because I have worked very hard to keep my personal biases and opinions out of this chapter, I have become more aware than ever before that God has strong thoughts on the subject. And he is not closed minded, nor is he a hater. As a matter of fact, God is very much a lover. His position on homosexuality is given not to squash the person who is trapped in a lifestyle of homosexuality, but to bring them freedom.

Remember, when looking at any issue, our standard can't be the personal opinion of someone we respect or look up to. It must be God's Word. So let's see what it says.

"For this reason a man will leave his father and mother and be united to his wife, and they will become one flesh" (Gen.

2:24). God's design is for man and woman to be joined in marriage.

"Therefore God gave them over in the sinful desires of their hearts to sexual impurity for the degrading of their bodies with one another. . . . Because of this, God gave them over to shameful lusts. Even their women exchanged natural relations for unnatural ones. In the same way the men also abandoned natural relations with women and were inflamed with lust for one another. Men committed indecent acts with other men, and received in themselves the due penalty for their perversion" (Rom. 1:24, 26–27). "Natural" relationships, ones God intended, were to be between men and women. Because of their sinful desires, people began to experiment. Because of dangerous lust, they went against God's design.

"Do you not know that the wicked will not inherit the kingdom of God? Do not be deceived: Neither the sexually immoral nor idolaters nor adulterers nor male prostitutes nor homosexual offenders nor thieves nor the greedy nor drunkards nor slanderers nor swindlers will inherit the kingdom of God. And that is what some of you were. But you were washed, you were sanctified, you were justified in the name of the Lord Jesus Christ and by the Spirit of our God" (1 Cor. 6:9–11). People who embrace an immoral lifestyle and continue to live in it won't inherit the kingdom of God. However, there is hope for those who are trapped. They can get free. People who used to be caught up in their perversions have been washed, sanctified, and justified in a relationship with Jesus.

"Flee from sexual immorality. All other sins a man commits are outside his body, but he who sins sexually sins against his own body. Do you not know that your body is a temple of the Holy Spirit, who is in you, whom you have received from God? You are not your own; you were bought at a price. Therefore honor God with your body" (1 Cor. 6:18–20). Sexual sin does more *internal* damage than other sins. It doesn't do any more *eternal* damage (all sins are equal in this regard), but sexual sin is against your own body. And if you're a Christian, your body isn't even yours. It's God's. The command here is to honor God with our bodies.

"If we confess our sins, he is faithful and just and will forgive us our sins and purify us from all unrighteousness" (1 John 1:9). Society says that certain sins are harder to forgive than others. If that's the case, some would believe that homosexuality is one of the most difficult, because in certain circles it's one of the most shocking. However, this isn't the case. Anyone caught up in this lifestyle can get free simply by asking forgiveness. God will grant it immediately.

"To him who is able to keep you from falling and to present you before his glorious presence without fault and with great joy—to the only God our Savior be glory, majesty, power and authority, through Jesus Christ our Lord, before all ages, now and forevermore! Amen" (Jude 24–25). This amazing Scripture tells us that God is able to keep us from falling and to present us without fault. This is a difficult thought for a person caught in a lifestyle of homosexuality to imagine. But anyone who surrenders to Christ, begins to rely on his strength, and adds self-discipline to that equation can get free. God has the ability to help them from falling and going back.

IT'S TIME TO CLIMB

As the attitude that homosexuality is a valid alternative gains momentum, more and more people are trapped in this lifestyle, know someone who is, or are beginning to consider it. God desperately wants to help everyone overcome these tendencies, not because he gets squeamish around something that makes him uncomfortable, but because he knows homosexuality carries with it severe consequences.

For that reason, I want to give you some practical suggestions that will help you get free from homosexuality, avoid it so it never affects you, or help someone else find freedom through Christ:

Understand God's view of homosexuality. It's clear that God opposes homosexuality in every form, but he clearly loves those who are ensnared by it. It's imperative that you allow God to fashion your opinions about the subject according to his Word instead of adopting bits and pieces of the world's view.

Many will argue that God made people gay, so they shouldn't fight it. Others who aren't knowledgeable on the subject will say that the Bible's view is unclear. And others will simply say that God's judgments are outdated. However, there's no way around it. Either you choose to believe what the Bible says or you declare that you disagree with God.

This may be a hard line to take, but it's the right one. "Let God be true, and every man a liar" (Rom. 3:4).

If needed, repent. Repentance is the first step toward getting free from anything that God deems a sin. By admitting to God that you've been living according to a standard other than his, you're asking for his forgiveness and help.

Turn from your involvement. As you may know, repentance also takes action. It takes movement—walking away from the sin and toward God. So although verbal (or prayerful) repentance is the first step, if you willfully walk back into sin, your repentance has been unproductive.

If you're in a relationship, you must break it off. It isn't right. If you're beginning to feel pulled toward someone of the same sex, you need to walk away from that relationship as well, at least until things change and you can rightfully control your emotions.

Confide in someone who will support you and pray for you. If you're at the beginning stages of breaking free from homosexuality's hold, then you're in for a tough battle. It's very possible to get free, but it will be difficult. That's why you need to find a friend (preferably someone older whom you trust both personally and spiritually) who will be there for you and help you win your war.

The initial conversation may be one of the most difficult you'll ever have, but once you break through, you'll have an ally who will be there for you. When you sense that you're struggling, you won't have to sit all alone wondering if you'll be able to make it. You can run to them, and they can help you in those dry and difficult times.

Flee temptation. God's order is always to flee from things that are dangerous for us (see 2 Tim. 2:22). For that reason, you must take evasive action. If your attitude toward homosexuality has become increasingly influenced by certain TV shows and movies, you need to stop watching them. Don't lie to yourself. They are not harmless. They are combating your convictions and trying to get you to adopt a philosophy that's contrary to God's.

Avoid dating for a while. If you're considering your sexual preferences, then you still have some internal stuff to work through. For that reason, dating (even people of the opposite gender) isn't wise. You'd be better off to give God a chunk of time to reveal himself to you. As you commit yourself to him in this way, you'll give him permission and access to heal your wounds, establish your identity, and strengthen your spiritual life.

Spend time with God. There's nothing better to help you overcome sin, convince you of your value, and help you discern God's truth than to invest in your relationship with God. As you make a habit out of reading his Word, praying, and learning to worship, the things in your life that God doesn't want there will begin to fall away. Every moment you spend in God's presence will go great distances toward helping you know who he is and who he made you to be. He created you for a purpose. He has a destiny, an identity, and a goal for your life. You'll move closer to those things as you spend time with him.

VIEW FROM THE TOP

Godly standards are for everyone. They bring God's blessing and place the obedient under his protection. For that reason, I had no choice but to be honest and broach this difficult subject.

God loves all people—even homosexuals. And I do as well. I refuse to let my personal preferences make me back down from someone who needs to know that God has something better for them. I can't stand by and watch as people are ensnared in a lifestyle that steals their joy, their self-worth, and their ability to relate to God.

With the same aggressiveness that our society encourages and protects the homosexual lifestyle, I must tell others of the love of Jesus. Won't you join me in doing damage to the devil's destructive plan by loving others enough to tell them the truth?

GAINING GROUND

Ask Yourself This—What are your opinions about homosexuality in light of what God's Word says? Does God have the ability to love the individual but hate their lifestyle? Do you? Have you ever dealt with feelings of homosexuality? Do you know someone who has? Do you believe that

God can help anyone overcome these issues? What advice would you give someone who is trapped in this lifestyle or is considering experimenting with it?

Key Scripture—"Do you not know that the wicked will not inherit the kingdom of God? Do not be deceived: Neither the sexually immoral nor idolaters nor adulterers nor male prostitutes nor homosexual offenders nor thieves nor the greedy nor drunkards nor slanderers nor swindlers will inherit the kingdom of God. And that is what some of you were. But you were washed, you were sanctified, you were justified in the name of the Lord Jesus Christ and by the Spirit of our God" (1 Cor. 6:9–11).

Ask God to Help—Because the issue of homosexuality is a spiritual topic and not simply hormonal or emotional, you have to work it through on a spiritual plane. You can do that by praying: *"God, I thank you that you created me perfectly. I wasn't a mistake, and I'm not missing something internal that you intended me to have. But I know that the devil would love to steal from me by perverting your plan for my life. I won't allow him to do that. God, would you protect me in my sexual identity? Don't allow me to do anything that wouldn't please you. God, if I've done anything or if I've even thought anything that's contrary to your plan for my life, forgive me and help me overcome those things. I thank you for your perfect, unconditional love for me. Amen."*

conclusion

"where am i?"

"Where am I?" That was what the look on April's face said as she climbed off the bus. The imprints in her skin made it clear that she'd been sleeping pretty soundly when we arrived at our destination. Although her eyes were open and her body was standing upright, her comprehension hadn't caught up with her physical condition. She was confused and groggy.

After a few moments, her wits finally began to return to her. She started to shake the sleep off, and she began to recall where we were and why we were there.

We had just journeyed for over an hour in an overcrowded bus to serve a church in a poor part of the country. The bus ride had lulled April to sleep, and it had also allowed her to forget about the work that lay ahead.

As the bus emptied, the young people were told to pick up the shovels and rakes and start moving rocks. With smiles on their faces, most of the teenagers gladly threw themselves into their tasks. However, April did not. She vocally expressed her lack of desire to work on such a hot day. Several times that day, she stated that she wished she was still back at the hotel sleeping. All day she murmured, complained, and protested.

After several of her peers picked up her attitude, I knew something had to be done. Pulling her aside, I reminded her that she'd chosen to participate in this excursion of her own free will. I told her that if she wasn't willing to make the necessary sacrifices, she shouldn't have even boarded the plane with us. Because she had frustrated me, I said very strongly, "You should've thought about the consequences of your decision before you decided to come."

Knowing that I was right, she walked away. For the rest of the day, she kept to herself. She did a little work but not much. However, I do think that it finally got through. She was where she was, and she was doing what she was doing of her own volition. She'd known what she was getting into, and she couldn't blame anyone but herself. It was her own decision that had put her in that position, and she was going to have to make the best of it.

Where are you heading?

Have you ever felt confused? Ever asked yourself, *How did I get here?* Maybe you were just like April and felt like you awoke to circumstances and surroundings that were unfamiliar and unattractive.

I know several people who have felt just like that. Somehow, they're surprised as they begin to evaluate where they are. Their confusion adds to their inability to take responsibility for what their lives look like.

Maybe they're twenty-five and they realize they have nothing to show for their lives except broken relationships and frustrated dreams. Maybe they're just graduating from high school and realize that their recreational drinking has turned into a personal demon of torment that continues to control their lives through alcoholism. Perhaps they realize for the first time that they're liars who have burned bridges as people have begun to discover their deceit.

No matter what the story, when people come to and realize that they don't like where they are, they struggle to get perspective and understanding. But, truthfully, they might not like what they see.

I'm convinced that very few things are out of our control. Our direction will be determined in large part by our everyday choices, the way we respond to God's conviction, and the way we battle for our integrity and character. Therefore, when you take an inventory of your life in a month, a year, five or ten years, or at the end of your life, if you don't like where you are, there will be no one to blame but yourself.

But if you look back and smile, you'll know it's because you made wise choices and worked with God to get to that place.

If you want to make sure that those self-inspection days are a pleasure and not a horrible shock, you must begin today. Don't wait until you get out of school or until you get married. Don't wait until you've sowed your wild oats and had your fun. Start today to work on the reputation you'll wear tomorrow. Invest today in your character.

HERE'S HOW

If you're going to like the person you become in future years, you're going to have to be intentional about two things in your life. Here is where it all begins:

You must approach God differently. Many Christians ignore God. They know he's there if they need him in a crisis, but they don't spend time with him regularly in a way that aids their spiritual development and helps them become more like him. If you want your life to be a testimony of all that God can do in an average life, you must fall in love with him and engage him in relationship daily. If you want your sin life to decrease and your commitment to holiness and purity to be distinguishing and noticeable factors, then you must come into his presence.

As you spend time with God through reading the Bible, learning to pray, and learning to offer up your heart in worship, God will invade your life and begin to give you victory over sin and draw you close to himself.

The real key here is spending time with him, but many people don't know how. If you feel like God is distant, and you really don't know how to connect with him, you might need to approach someone who has been walking with God longer and ask them for help. If you get frustrated because you don't have a lot of discipline and your mind tends to wander as you try to meet God in the quiet place, don't get discouraged. Find a mentor or a teacher who can assist you in learning how to let God saturate your heart and captivate your attention.

The bottom line is that if you really want to live for God and be all that he wants you to be, you must spend time with him. If you do, you'll build momentum on your way toward growth. If you don't, it's just a matter of time until you hit another dip in the road and lose ground.

You must approach the world differently. This book is centered on this theme. We can't live as the world does and expect to mature in God. We can't adopt its philosophies and expect to please God or become more like him.

It's time that Christians draw a line in the sand and declare that they are stepping over it. We must move from the shallow, self-gratifying, and sinful side over to the pure, holy, committed, and devoted side. On the one side, we fight for our rights and live for ourselves. But on the other, we want what God wants and are willing to take drastic measures to protect our spiritual walk. The one side is filled with dips, depressions, and drop-offs, but the other ensures a steady climb toward God.

Knowing God's standards is one thing. Obeying them is another. Knowing that God's ways are protected is good. But surrendering to his plan is better. It isn't enough to know God's intentions; we must adopt them as our own. If we're unwilling, we're fooling ourselves.

Although April woke up and was disappointed with where she was going to spend her day, we'll one day awake to a more serious realization. We'll discover where we are and what we have become. What everyone else has known for some time will become evident to us. What we have built will finally be visible. Are you going to be surprised and disappointed? Or, with intentional effort and a determined direction, will that day be pleasing to you?

It's your decision. Choose wisely.

Gaining Ground

Ask Yourself This—If I continue going in the same direction, what will my life look like in five years? Will I be moral or immoral? Will I be dominated by certain sins, or will I be working toward freedom? What does my devotional life need to look like if I'm going to build momentum in my pursuit of God? Do I really know how to connect with God? Is there someone I need to ask to teach me how to meet with God? Was there a certain topic addressed in this book that I really need to work on? Which one?

Key Scripture—"To him who is able to keep you from falling and to present you before his glorious presence without fault and with great joy—to the only God our Savior be glory, majesty, power and authority, through Jesus Christ our Lord, before all ages, now and forevermore! Amen" (Jude 24–25).

Ask God to Help—Let's close this book in prayer: *"God, I can't thank you enough for the way you love me and all that you do for me. But the most exciting thing to me is that you really want a relationship with me. Would you teach me how to walk with you? Would you help me understand how to approach you so that I really am building a strong and intimate relationship? I need your help in so many areas,* *and I give you permission to help me know when I'm doing something you aren't pleased with. Help me protect myself from things that would affect my walk with you. I love you, and I give all that I am to you again. In the name of your Son I pray. Amen."*

notes

Chapter 5: What to Do When All Hope Is Gone

1. Julie Monahan, "True Stories Dealing with Depression," *Teen* Magazine, October 1993, 42.

Chapter 7: Ambushing Innocence

1. Dr. Jennings Bryant study, cited by Victor B. Cline, "Correlating Adolescent and Adult Exposure to Sexually Explicit Material and Sexual Behavior" (paper presented to the Attorney General's commission on pornography in 1986).

2. Ibid.

3. Josh McDowell and Bob Hostetler, *Right from Wrong; What You Need to Know to Help Youth Make Right Choices* (Dallas: Word, 1994), 258.

Chapter 8: It Only Takes One

1. Reported in *Group Members Only,* cited in *Josh McDowell Research Almanac and Statistical* Digest (Josh McDowell Ministry, 1990), 147.

2. *Monitoring the Future.* National Adolescent Student Health Survey, 1987. Cited in "It is Time to Ban the Advertising of Alcohol from Broadcasting," *AFA Journal,* January 1990, 12.

3. Ibid.

4. Ibid.

5. Ibid.

6. Jerry Johnston, *Why Suicide?* (Nashville: Oliver Nelson, 1987), 54.

Chapter 9: A Real Threat

1. Jay Kesler and Ronald A. Beers, *Parents and Teenagers* (Colorado Springs: Chariot Victor, 1984), 502.

2. Linda Stahl, "Kids Know Drugs but Not Risks," *USA Today*, 13 September 1989, DI.

3. Dan Speiling, "Teen Drug Use Drops, but Users Get 'Very High,' " *USA Today*, 27 September, 1989, DI.

4. Johnston, *Why Suicide?* 63.

5. McDowell and Hostetler, *Right from Wrong*, 6.

6. "How to Beat Drugs," *U.S. News and World Report*, 14 August 1989, 70.

7. McDowell and Hostetler, *Right from Wrong*, 9.

Chapter 11: Protecting Your Purity

1. Cited in Jeannie Echenique, "Early Dating May Lead to Early Sex," *USA Today*, 12 November 1986, D1.

Sean Dunn is the founder and director of Champion Ministries, an outreach that works to creatively and effectively communicate God's Word, his love, and his purpose with people between the ages of twelve and twenty-four. He is the former youth director of a church in Castle Rock, Colorado, where he resides with his wife and four children.

For a free newsletter and a list of materials from Champion Ministries or for information on having Sean Dunn minister at your church, conference, retreat, school, or other ministry group, please contact the ministry at:

Sean Dunn
c/o Champion Ministries
P.O. Box 1323
Castle Rock, CO 80104

Phone: 303-660-3582
E-mail: champion@championministries.org